W9-DHM-650

How to care for
SHADE and
ORNAMENTAL
TREES

WITHDRAWN

By Dr. John P. Baumgardt

Contents

Introduction

Who needs a book on tree care? The lucky person finding himself with his new home on an undeveloped lot requires guidance on proper selection of trees, proper placement of trees, proper sizes of trees to buy. The homeowner with a well developed planting, including trees and shrubs, needs information on fertilizing his woody plants, on the best way and the best time to prune his trees, what to do about disease and insect problems. As a matter of fact, everybody with a garden needs a book on tree care.

To be really useful, such a book needs to present sound information. There must be diagrams showing details of tree care; planting, watering, fertilizing, pruning, and so on. There need to be lists and tables, all that "dry" data, condensed factual information, that tells a puzzled tree owner exactly what he wishes to know. Garden books today tend to speak in generalities because New York publishers believe that facts scare off potential buyers. The truth is, gardeners with a problem look for books with facts, books that specifically define **their** problems and suggest definitive steps to alleviate the difficulty.

This volume, then, presents facts, illustrations, lists, and tables intended to help any person with trees in his garden. The Do's and Don't are all here. But there is more. There is enough basic botany to tell a curious gardener why he should apply phosphate fertilizers when setting a new tree and why not apply complete fertilizers until the tree is established. There is sufficient botany to make clear how roots grow and how leaves function. This botanical information supplies the logic on which the various horticultural practices are based. It is the "why" that follows the "how."

Certain practices are stressed over and over again in this book. Often the emphasis lies on a "do not." This is not because of a negative attitude, but is a calculated way of sidetracking wide-spread gardening practices that give poor results. It seems logical to heavily fertilize a newly planted tree and to water it every day or so. But heavy fertilizing stimulates exceptionally leafy growth which puts an undue strain on an unestablished root system, and frequent watering oversaturates the soil, driving out critical oxygen, and killing roots. Commonly accepted mal-practices get a big X in this volume.

American gardeners no longer are satisfied with commonplace trees. Why plant an everyday pin oak when the cultivar "Sovereign" offers so much more style? There's no reason to continuously shear a seedling tree into a formal globe-shape, when you can buy a built-up tree that makes a ball head naturally. Lists of specially shaped and of grafted forms are included to help every gardener know what is available. If the tree that seems to meet your needs is not to be found in a local nursery, check with the nearest botanic garden or arboretum — they can tell you who sells that sort mail-order. As the demand increases, it will become worth while for local nurseries to handle newer items.

Who needs a book on tree care? Everybody who owns a piece of property or who gardens where trees grow needs the information that is found in this book.

CHAPTER 1
How to select a tree

TREES IN THE GARDEN

Provide shade

Give privacy

Furnish
a vertical
dimension

Modify
the environment

as windbreaks

as sound buffers

as natural
air conditioners

Create seasonal
beauty

with flowers

with fruits

with foliage color

When you buy a tree . . . points to consider

Trees dominate the garden. A fine, mature tree may set the tone for the entire landscape. From a design standpoint, trees furnish the vertical dimension; lawns, beds, and borders are relatively low but trees tower overhead. They are to the landscape what pillars, walls, and roofs are to architecture. They furnish the dimension of height.

Aside from beauty, grandeur, and similar aesthetic aspects, trees offer the gardener and his garden several practical virtues. Trees affect the weather; they break the wind, provide shade, and in summer provide natural air conditioning because their leaves evaporate tremendous amounts of water and evaporation is a cooling process.

The sun-drenched garden is limited to ornamental species which thrive in full sun. Add a tree or two and the gardener's palette is enriched with shade loving plants and those that require partial shade.

Large-growing trees usually are classed as shade trees. Smaller sorts usually planted for colorful flowers, bright fruits, or especially attractive leaves often are grouped as ornamental trees. Sometimes this category is further subdivided into flowering trees (for example, dogwoods, hawthorns and flowering crabapple trees) and ornamental trees (birches, Japanese maples, oleasters—all with attractive bark or leaves or form). But these distinctions become blurred.

In Southern gardens no flower could be more important or more beautiful than the great, fragrant white blossoms of the bullbay magnolia, but the tree, soaring to sixty feet or so, certainly qualifies as a shade tree. In the Pacific Northwest the madrone tree's bright cinnamon-colored bark is an ornamental asset; but in that misty, cool climate, the dappled shade of a madrone is all a garden needs. Middle Westerners plant the golden rain-tree for its mid-summer panicles of yellow flowers—and when the high crowned, graceful trees are twenty years old they sit beneath them.

Why are you planting a tree?

Your mind is made up. You are going to buy a tree for the garden. Is it to be a shade tree or will it be a flowering sort? Is it to become a formal feature on the lawn or will it become part of the "garden wall", that bank of living greenery that gives your garden privacy and shelter? There are several factors to consider before settling on a particular sort of tree.

Good landscape design calls for proper placement of the various elements of the garden. Proportion is another critical consideration. The character of the garden determines location and choice of plant materials, including trees. Most design experts agree that the average city lot needs only one or two very large trees, with various flowering and ornamental trees worked in as the design develops. From a practical standpoint, where summers are hot, try to plan your design so the tree will shade the house through the middle of the day.

There are pitfalls to avoid. A favorite technique of house builders is to include in the cost of construction a generous amount for "landscaping." This money usually becomes part of the builder's profit, with only a very small fraction dedicated to grading, sodding, and inevitably, two trees planted midway between the street and the house in the front lawn. These two "front yard" trees have almost become a trademark of American suburbia. Such formal placement seldom fits into any scheme of good landscaping.

If you are planting a tree, place it where it benefits the house, the sitting terrace, or the garden design. Never select a large-growing tree if your planting site is near utility wires. Trees and overhead lines do not mix, and as power and telephones generally come first in the scheme of things, your tree must be of a sort that never will imperil the wires.

Before heading for the nursery analyze your reasons for planting a tree. If the tree is to provide shade for a woodsy garden it must have deep roots that will not interfer with your fragile ferns and woodland flowering plants. If it is to develop into a living umbrella for the house or terrace it must have a high, spreading crown—a low-branching sort is out of the question. If it is to block the view of an outdoor movie screen across the road it must be low-branching and dense, sufficiently twiggy to provide a visual barrier winter and summer.

Perhaps you are thinking in terms of ornamental value. Your garden is too green; a largish mass of another color seems desirable. Will it be oleaster, with its silvery white foliage, one of the Japanese maples with bronze or purplish-red leaves or something even more sprightly such as the variegated Norway maple or one of the variegated box-elders?

Your nurseryman is likely to want to know about your soil; does it drain rapidly? Is it loamy or backfill clay? Is the planting site low and sheltered or will your tree have to stand up to gusty summer winds? All of these factors enter into selection.

Decide exactly what your tree is to do for you and for your garden, define size limitations, exposure, soil conditions and other environmental factors, and then talk trees with the nurseryman.

Pitfalls of tree placement

Wrong - Never plant paired trees midway between street and house

Wrong - Never plant a tall or large growing tree near utility lines

Size makes a difference

Instant landscaping is a relatively common practice today. Machines roar in and shove the earth about, sod is laid, beds and borders are laid out, turned and planted, holes are dug for trees big enough to sit under, and there it is, a "finished" garden, almost overnight. Unfortunately, in most cases these instant gardens look their best the day they are completed and their subsequent history is one of continuous deterioration.

On the other hand, the garden that builds slowly, with plants put in at the proper season in sizes that move readily and establish quickly, gets better each year. While it is perfectly possible to dig up and move full sized trees, the expense and wear and tear on the tree seldom warrants such a practice.

For example, here is an actual case; a landscape job was underway and several twenty-five foot tall pin oak trees (these move readily), nursery grown, were available for the job, and were moved in with great care. To save money and to complete the planting they were interplanted with broomstick-sized pin oaks. After ten years the large trees still had not recovered sufficiently from shock to resume growth; they are alive but that is all, and they are filled with small dead branches indicating insufficient root systems. The broomstick-sized trees are vigorous and thriving and match the older ones, size for size.

That is an important lesson to learn. While we can move plants of almost any size, beyond certain reasonable limits it is a poor practice. Modest sized trees, moved at the correct season and planted properly, resume growth quickly and with care make rapid growth.

Avoid "fast-growing trees"

Never ask your nurseryman for a "fast-growing" tree. He has them for people who do not know any better. Rather, ask for the sturdiest possible sort of tree, one that is a real asset to the garden, move it in a suitable size, and after it has had a year or two to get its roots down, begin to push it with judiciously applied tree fertilizer and seasonal watering. It will grow just about as fast as you could wish.

And that is another important lesson. The so-called fast growing trees, the Siberian elms, hybrid elms, soft or silver maples, poplars, and the like, grow rapidly, ruining the garden with their surface roots, and they die quickly as in almost every case their wood is weak and their life span is brief. Buy a modest sized tree of the best sort and go from there.

Factors favoring planting

Factor
Climate
Soil
Variety
Season

Bare root versus balled and burlap-wrapped

A tree dug with a ball of soil carefully held in place with a burlap wrapping costs quite a bit more than a tree bought with its roots bare. Is the difference in price warranted? It all depends. Climate makes a great deal of difference. For instance, in the cool, misty Pacific Northwest quite large trees, and quite fragile trees—such as the delicate Japanese cherries—are moved bare root with almost no loss. Because the soil tends to be almost uniformly damp, and the air is cool, moisture laden, top growth resumes slowly, and the development of new roots keeps pace with leafy growth.

A deficit never develops where a heavily leaved crown demands far more water on a hot, windy

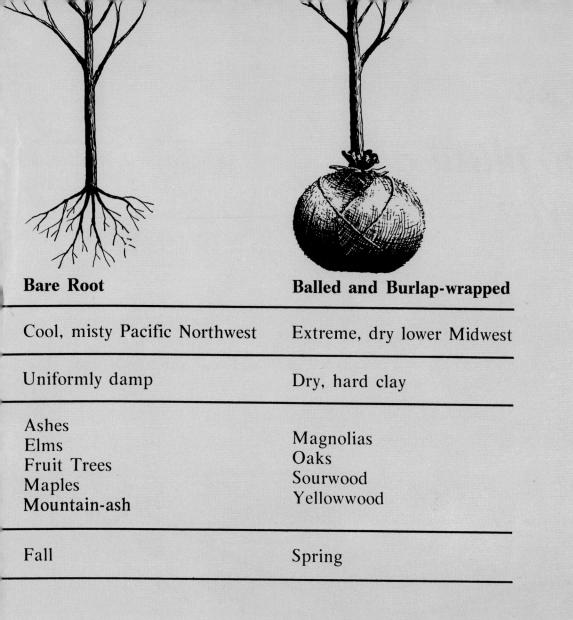

Bare Root	Balled and Burlap-wrapped
Cool, misty Pacific Northwest	Extreme, dry lower Midwest
Uniformly damp	Dry, hard clay
Ashes Elms Fruit Trees Maples Mountain-ash	Magnolias Oaks Sourwood Yellowwood
Fall	Spring

summer day than an unestablished root system can supply. On the other hand, in the lower Middle West it has become fashionable to move almost all trees in the balled and burlapped condition. The planting season begins in very early fall, runs through the winter stopping only for a few days now and again when the soil is frozen, and continues through the spring well into warm weather. Few trees are lost. Obviously, climate makes a difference.

The time of year makes a difference, too. Generally speaking, woody plants should be moved in the dormant (leafless) condition. Where winters are not too severe fall transplanting is best. Early spring is second choice and is recommended for areas with harsh winter weather. Tree roots grow throughout the winter months when the soil is not frozen. If you plant your new tree in the fall root growth will begin soon and will continue through much of the winter so that when buds open in spring a partially reestablished root system will be able to support the new growth.

On the other hand, when a tree is moved in spring buds open soon, leafy shoots emerge, and the root system may be hard put to supply sufficient water to keep the top of the plant from wilting. Heavy watering will not help because the roots just are not there to take it in.

Some species with sparse root systems or with root systems that do not heal and begin regrowth quickly always should be moved with a ball of soil. The magnolias fall into this category. Some of the native oaks, sweetgum, sourwood, and yellowwood seem to require the ball and burlap treatment for best results. On the other hand, the elms, ashes, maples, mountain-ashes, most fruit trees and many other sorts move perfectly well in the bare root condition so long as certain conditions are met.

If cost is a consideration, by all means, buy bare root, do a first rate job of planting the tree, nurture it carefully, and chances are that in ten years it will be as large or larger than a balled specimen planted the same time.

CHAPTER 2
How to plant your tree

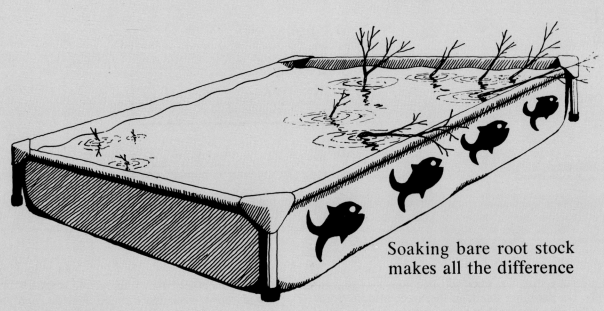

Soaking bare root stock
makes all the difference

Bare root trees

Soak entire tree for 24 hours

Dig a hole broader and deeper than the tree's root system

Prepare fill soil according to directions on following pages

Hold tree, roots in hole, and toss loose fill soil around the roots

Flood the hole to settle the soil (continue to support the tree)

Stake the tree, work remaining soil into watering saucer

Folding back and burying burlap
from top of ball stock makes
all the difference

Balled and
burlap-wrapped trees

Dig a hole 50% wider and slightly deeper than tree ball.

Loosen soil in bottom hole, add fertilizer and soil amendments as directed on following pages. Cover with prepared fill soil, adjust soil level so top of tree ball is flush with surrounding ground.

Set tree in hole, adjust to stand vertically, half fill with prepared fill soil, cut cords, and fold back burlap.

Complete filling hole, settle with water, work remaining soil into watering. Guy or stake the tree.

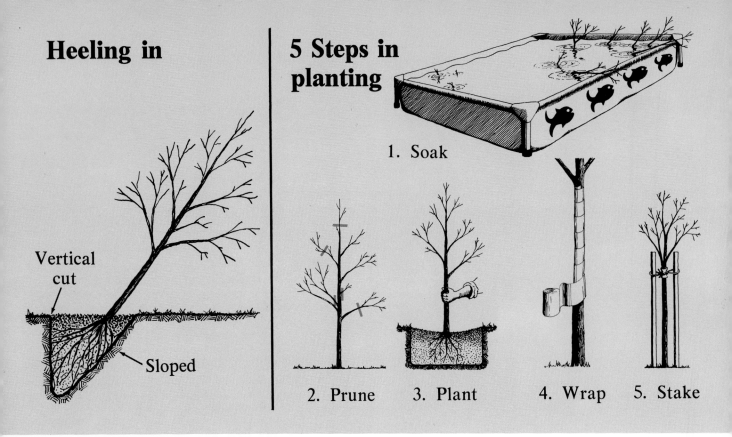

Heeling in

Vertical cut

Sloped

5 Steps in planting

1. Soak

2. Prune

3. Plant

4. Wrap

5. Stake

Plant your tree in soil that is crumbly-moist. Never try to plant in soggy soil; if the tree arrives during a rainy spell, heel it in until the soil is workable. To heel in a bare root tree, spade out a trench large enough to take the root system with no crowding. One side of the trench should be vertical, the other should be sloping. Lay the tree in the trench with the trunk supported by the sloping side of the trench. Mound the soil taken from the trench over the roots, covering them entirely. If the tree has to be held for very long, strew a generous layer of straw or hay over the trench **and** tree top to cut down on drying.

To hold a balled tree, set it in a shady place and pack the ball with a thick mass of straw and hay, protecting sides and top.

The planting hole

A properly dug planting hole is roomy, with good bottom drainage. Old timers say "never plant a five dollar tree in a fifty cent hole." This makes considerable sense. Your tree is an investment. You expect it to take hold quickly and to resume growing soon. You want that sapling to become a fine flowering specimen or a graceful shade tree within a reasonable time. The top of the tree will grow just as fast as its root system permits, and the vigor of the root system depends on the planting hole and surrounding soil. Do the best possible job of planting your tree.

Planting a bare root tree

Five steps are involved here. Soak the tree, prune it, plant it, wrap it, and stake it. Bare root trees usually are dug in the fall to be held in cold storage over winter. Never accept a tree with bark that is shrivelled or one with dry roots. The bark should be juicy, green when scraped, and the roots should be crisp, flexible, and distinctly damp to the touch.

Even so, the tree needs to take up more water before planting. In the old days this was no trouble. Most trees arrived bare root and the gardener shook them from their wrappings and plunged them roots, tops, and all, in the horse trough while holes were dug. Today horse troughs are few, but the need for total submerging of bare root trees is just as pressing.

Plunge your tree in a fish pond—yours or the neighbor's. Or gently bend the top around and sink the tree in the bathtub. A final alternative is to dig a tree length trench in the garden, line it with a sheet of plastic to make a temporary pool, and put the tree to soak. Twelve hours underwater is barely enough, twenty-four hours is just right, and more than thirty hours is dangerous.

While your tree is soaking, dig the hole. By now you have an idea of the root spread of the tree and also its depth. Make your planting hole at least a foot wider than the natural spread of the roots and some deeper. The depth of the hole partially depends on soil structure. If your soil is well drained, average loam you have no problem. But if it is heavy, soggy

Planting hole check list

___ **Width** - 12" wider than natural spread
___ **Depth** - No deeper than previous depth markings on trunk
___ **Sides** - Vertical
___ **Bottom** - Loosen soil for downward drainage
___ **Fertilizer** - 2 cups 5-10-5 worked in with organic debris and covered 2" at bottom only. Cover with fill soil.

Fill ingredients

1/3 organic—peat, leafmold, manure

1/4 cup of 20% superphosphate per bushel

Add sand if heavy clay

DON'T add nitrate or ammonium salts

---

clay, or if the bottom of the hole extends into tight subsoil, by all means dig deeper, work in quantities of coarse compost, damp peat, leafmold or other partially decomposed organic debris along with a generous scattering (two cupfuls per three foot diameter hole) of 5-10-5 fertilizer.

Work the organic debris and the fertilizer through the loosened subsoil and then—this is important—cover with at least two inches of prepared fill soil and tramp it down. New roots never should come in contact with fertilizers; that buried fertilizer and the organic matter will work together to convert the soggy subsoil or clay into faster draining, loamy soil. The covering of fill soil keeps roots from getting into the fertilizer where they might be injured.

Examine the soil taken from the planting hole. If it is good quality garden loam it is suitable to use for planting soil as is. If it is really bad stuff, graded out clay from the basement excavation or something similar, discard it and replace with loam. If it is just so-so, clumpy, hard, but workable, modify it with peat and sand. Almost any soil is improved by adding an organic material such as peat or leafmold because these materials improve soil texture, making the soil spongy, better aerated, yet more water retentive while fast draining.

The organic additives lighten heavy soils and give body to sandy or silt soils. As much as one-third (volume) of peat or leafmold may be added to your fill soil. If the soil is very heavy think of adding sand, too. Try to estimate the volume of your fill soil and mix into it about one-fourth cupful of 20% superphosphate per bushel. Superphosphate is relatively insoluble and offers little danger to roots. But it does gradually release phosphates into the soil and phosphate is the chemical most responsible for vigorous root growth.

By adding phosphate at planting time you are insuring quick establishment of your tree. Do not use fertilizers containing nitrates or ammonium salts as these chemicals encourage heavy leafy growth, and a vigorous top growth on a newly set plant puts too much strain on the water absorbing capacity of the roots. Complete fertilizers come later on. In rural areas OLD, well-decayed barnyard manure substitutes very well for peat or leafmold; but never use fresh or only partially decomposed animal manures. Never use dehydrated manure out of a bag for tree planting because this may be "hot", that is, yielding too much growth stimulating mineral when moistened. But bagged, dehydrated manure is a very good thing to work into the bottom of the hole before a protecting layer of unfertilized fill soil is added.

With the hole prepared and the fill soil ready, it is time to plant the tree. Your tree should go into the soil so it is at the same depth at which it grew originally. Probably it will settle somewhat following planting, so set it an inch or two high (depending on depth of hole) to allow for subsidence. In any case, it is better to end up slightly on the shallow side than on the deep side.

Before planting the tree, let's do some pruning. Stand the tree in its water bath, roots still covered, and prune the top. Make all cuts on a forty-five degree angle with a healthy bud at the apex of the cut. Remove all spindly twigs from the trunk and main branches. Remove crowding branches. Now you should have an uncluttered tree with a sturdy leader

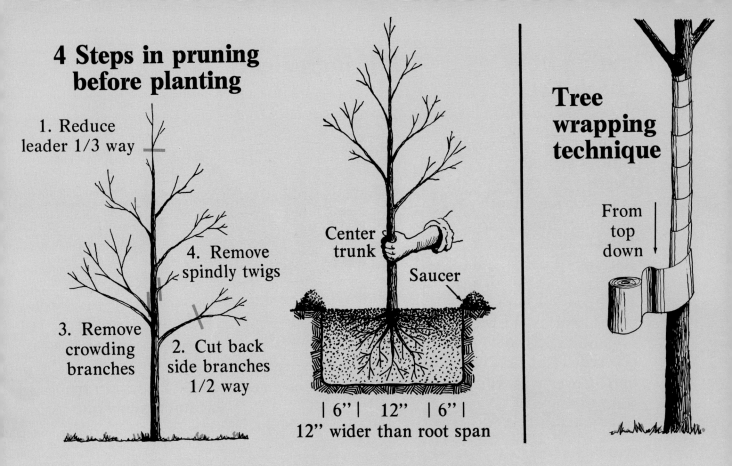

4 Steps in pruning before planting

1. Reduce leader 1/3 way

4. Remove spindly twigs

3. Remove crowding branches

2. Cut back side branches 1/2 way

Center trunk

Saucer

| 6" | 12" | 6" |
12" wider than root span

Tree wrapping technique

From top down

(the main, upright shoot) and well-spaced side branches. Cut back the side branches half way and reduce the leader by about one-third. This seems severe. But remember, your tree has lost a great part of its root system during digging; this rather stringent top pruning brings back a balance between roots and top, and as a result the plant will reestablish more quickly and the lost branches will be quickly restored in a season or two.

After pruning the top, quickly prune the roots, merely cutting back all broken or otherwise injured roots. **Do not allow those roots to dry out.**

Hold the tree in the center of the hole at the appropriate height, and with a shovel work quickly to throw fine soil through the naturally spread roots, filling in around them. It helps if two persons are involved, one holding the tree and the other wielding the shovel. But one man can do it. When the roots are covered, jump in the hole and gingerly walk down the soil to squeeze out trapped air as air pockets are fatal to roots.

This is quite satisfactory for fall planting. But there is a better way when planting bare root stock in the spring. Flood the hole and let the water soak away. The water does a fine job of settling the earth tightly around the roots. But you will have to support the plant throughout the soaking process so it does not sway and pull roots out of position, and this is rather time consuming.

With soil compacted around the roots, complete filling the hole. There should be some excess soil.

Toss all the soil into a broad cone with the tree trunk at its center. Now, gently rake the soil away, working round and round the tree, until you have created a broad, shallow saucer with its rim just inside the lip of the original hole. Take care not to scar the tree trunk through this operation.

Before settling the final fill soil with water, stake and wrap the tree. Wrapping comes first. The bark of young trees is thin, susceptible to sunburn. Older trees with mature, corrugated bark may be subjected to borer attack. A newly moved tree is a weakened tree, and wrapping is highly recommended. Buy commercial tree wrap from the garden shop or nurseryman. Begin at the bottom of the tree and unroll the band of paper, spiral fashion, overlapping to ensure full coverage and tight enough so slipping will not occur. Carry the wrapping up the trunk and beyond the lowest branches. Secure it with a piece of twine. Probably the tree wrap will weather away in about eighteen months or so. It needs to be in place for at least a year. Check from time to time to be sure a tie cord is not girdling the tree due to increase in trunk diameter. Some experts wrap from the top downwards—it makes little difference so long as the wrapping is securely in place.

With the tree wrap in place, stake the tree. There are several ways. The idea of staking is to prevent the tree from rocking back and forth, tearing off newly formed roots every time the wind blows. A slender, whippy tree needs only a sturdy wooden or metal stake driven vertically two or three inches from the trunk. Do not tie the tree directly to the stake.

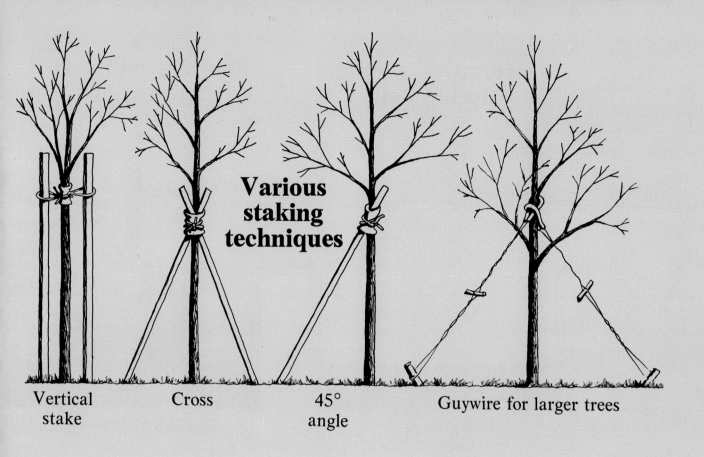

Various staking techniques

Vertical stake   Cross   45° angle   Guywire for larger trees

Rather, use soft cord or strips of rag to make a tie resembling a number 8 with the tree trunk through one hole and the stake through the other.

Where winds are strong and persistent, drive a heavy stake at about a forty-five degree angle (the base of the stake should just clear the planting hole; the top crossing the trunk of the tree four feet or so above the ground). With soft cord or strips of rag secure the tree trunk to the stake. **The stake should head into the wind.** Another advantage of this technique is that the stake is out of the root zone of the tree. There is no root disturbance when the stake is put in or when it is removed.

Pegs, guywires and turnbuckles are used for supporting larger trees. In a circle some four to eight feet from the trunk of the tree drive three to six sturdy pegs (two foot lengths of 2 x 4's turned edgewise toward the tree are good) angling them away from the tree at about thirty degrees. Stretch strong, fairly flexible wires from the stakes to the tree; these wires should loop the tree trunk about half way from the ground to the tip of the tree.

Before securing the loop around the tree, slip a foot long piece of old garden hose over each wire and adjust this on the side of the tree opposite the peg to keep the taut wire from cutting the tree bark. With all the wires in place and reasonably snug, cut them midway between peg and tree, and insert a turnbuckle in each. Turn the turnbuckle so the pull on each wire is equal. From time to time check the tension on the wires and adjust it by turning the turnbuckles.

With the tree wrapped and staked or guyed, water it thoroughly. Fill the saucer with water and let it soak away. Fill it at least once more; if the water runs away quickly at the second filling, add water at least one more time.

Make up a schedule to help you keep track of watering intervals. It is tempting to overwater a newly planted tree, particularly if it wilts down at midday on a hot, windy day. But soggy soil only rots the roots, and does nothing but damage to the tree. The soil needs to be moderately damp, never soggy. On average soil, a thorough watering once each week when the rainfall is less than one inch is plenty. On heavy clay that stays wetter, watering at ten day intervals suffices. Where the soil is sandy, after four or five days dig down inside the rim of the soil saucer and if the soil seems dry at four inches, apply water. Each time you water soak the soil deeply.

There is another sort of watering that is beneficial. When your newly planted tree has leafed out on hot or windy days go out several times and with the hose nozzle set for a very fine mist syringe the foliage. This water bath cools the leaves and slows water loss from inside the tree. (Plant leaves have many tiny pores in their "skin" that allows water to be lost through evaporation and if water is evaporating from the leaves faster than roots can replace it the plant wilts, and prolonged or severe wilting leads to death.) In the Prairie and Great Plains states where the winds are hot, dry, and incessant, frequent syringing of tree foliage can mean the difference between successful establishment of a newly planted tree or its loss.

Anatomy of a good planting hole

Planting balled and burlap-wrapped tree

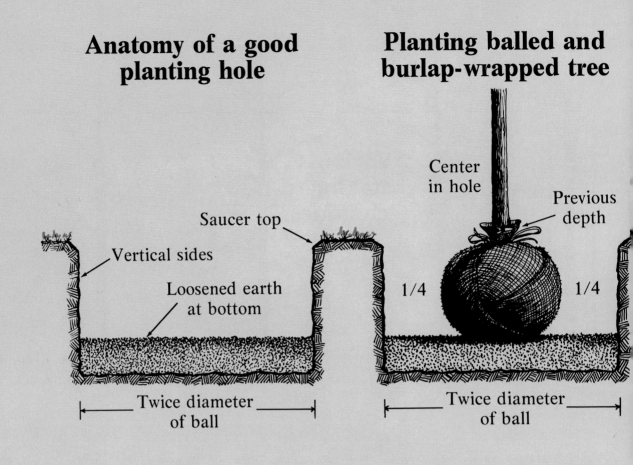

Saucer top

Vertical sides

Loosened earth at bottom

Twice diameter of ball

Center in hole

Previous depth

1/4   1/4

Twice diameter of ball

Planting a balled and burlap-wrapped tree

Handle your balled and burlap-wrapped tree gently. The whole point in paying a fancy price for that chunk of real estate clinging to the tree's roots is to protect the root system and to preserve the tiny, water absorbing roots that invariably are lost when a tree is moved in a bare root state. If the soil ball is cracked, for all practical purposes the tree is then a bare root tree with the roots enclosed in a burlap bag of soil. Never accept from the nursery a balled tree with a soggy ball or a loose ball. The soil ball should be firm, damp, and absolutely intact.

Having determined the planting site for your balled tree, measure the diameter of the ball. Mark out a hole twice the diameter of the soil ball. If, for example, the ball is eighteen inches across, dig a thirty-six inch wide hole. Does that sound excessive? It is not. With the ball centered in the hole there will be only nine inches of clearance around it.

Proceed as if you were making a hole for a bare root tree; that is, provide for downward drainage, loosening and correcting soil in the bottom of the hole if necessary. Provide a quantity of good quality fill soil to go into the hole around the soil ball. The surface of the tree ball should be flush with the surface of the surrounding soil when the planting job is finished. Because of the weight of a balled and burlap wrapped tree you must provide for settling if the bottom of the hole has been loosened for aeration and drainage correction. Build up a slight mound of soil in the center of the hole to support the tree; the top of the ball should be slightly higher than the surrounding soil. It will settle down an inch or two in a short time.

With the burlap in place, gently lower the tree into the hole. Center it. If your winds generally come from one direction, turn the heaviest branches in that direction because as the tree grows most growth will occur on the side away from the wind. Check to be sure the trunk is vertical, that the tree is centered, and that the ball is slightly raised unless it is resting on undisturbed soil. Now, shovel pulverized soil prepared with peat and superphosphate as discussed under bare root trees until the hole is filled almost to the shoulder of the ball.

Reach across and cut the cords or bands around the trunk and across the top of the ball. With a sharp knife slit the burlap across the top of the ball. Fold back the burlap so the top of the ball is exposed, and bury the burlap that is spread over the fill soil. Flood the hole, adding water until no more bubbles arise from around the ball, then complete filling the hole, and work the excess soil into a

Cut and loosen burlap wrapping

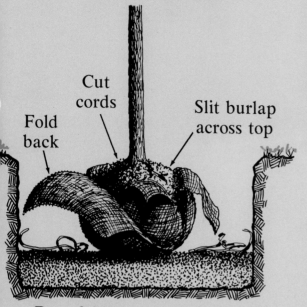

Cut cords

Slit burlap across top

Fold back

Bury folded back burlap with top soil

After care of a newly planted tree

Whether you plant your tree in fall or spring, whether it is balled or bare root, it is a hospital case for at least the first full summer, and probably will be weak for two or three years. If it is more than four inches in diameter, it will need nursing for five to ten years. Water at regular intervals. Apply no fertilizer of any sort during the first growing season. The superphosphate you added to the fill soil supplies the tree's needs for phosphate. Other nutrients might be detrimental. If the new growth of the tree is yellowish add a chelated iron compound (such as Sequestrene or Fe-Tracin) as instructed on the package. Generally this special form of iron can be dissolved in water and poured over the surface of the soil inside the watering saucer to be carried down when next the tree is watered.

As mentioned above, on hot, windy days syringe the tree's foliage with a very fine mist of water to reduce transpiration loss. If the tree persists in wilting on hot days, prune all green shoots back half way and take out entirely some of those that have developed inside the branching pattern. This removal of succulent green tissue balances the top of the tree to the root system and gives the tree a better chance for survival.

If your tree is fall planted, after a light crust of frost indicates that the soil is chilled enough to dis-

CAUTION

Apply no fertilizer during first growing season

Superphosphate at planting suffices

courage top growth apply a deep mulch of porous material such as straw, old hay, or leaves of a sort that do not mat down such as well dried and curled oak leaves. This mulch layer—it needs to be at least six inches deep and a foot is better—prevents freezing and thawing, and it enables the root system to continue growing for a much longer time. Probably it should be removed entirely, or at least raked off and fluffed up before replacing in mid-spring.

If your new tree comes through the first summer in good shape, early the second spring you can think about pushing it into faster growth with fertilizer. But if it was slow to establish, alive but struggling, do not fertilize at all, or at best, apply only a very light feeding. Use tree fertilizer cartridges in a hose attached tree root feeder and follow the instructions on the package. The best fertilizer formulation for a weak and struggling tree is a "transplant" or "take hold" type.

watering saucer as described in the bare root tree planting section.

Somebody is bound to ask why the burlap should be removed from the top of the ball and not from the sides and bottom. There is no good way to take burlap from the entire ball without the risk of having the soil ball crumble or crack. On the other hand, if any of the burlap remains on top of the soil ball and for one reason or another becomes exposed to the surface it acts as a wick in a kerosene lamp. That is, water evaporates quickly from the exposed portions, drawing more water from the buried burlap which in turn takes more water from the adjacent soil. The net result is a narrow, bone dry "pot" of soil at the ball-burlap-fill soil interface through which roots will not penetrate. The tree will die during hot, windy weather. **Never** leave burlap in place over the top of a planted tree or shrub. Always loosen it after the ball is securely socketed with fill soil and bury it two or three inches below the surface.

The balled and burlap-wrapped tree, when in the ground and with a water saucer raked out above is handled just as a bare root tree. Wrap the trunk with tree wrap paper. Guy the tree (**Never drive a stake through the soil ball**) or drive stakes, two or three of them, at the rim of the planting hole and cross tie the trunk with soft cord or rag strips. This tree, too, needs water about once a week when rainfall is less than one inch.

CHAPTER 3
How to fertilize your tree

Apply only a mild application of a transplant fertilizer to newly planted trees.

Fertilize trees planted less than 3 years very lightly.

Fertilize established trees every 3 to 5 years as recommended on the following pages.

If your tree is injured - hail storm, insect attack, air pollution damage - apply foliar fertilizer for quick stimulation.

Fertilize generally, at beginning of growing season. Never fertilize after midsummer.

If your tree is chlorotic (with yellow foliage when leaves should be green) fertilize with iron preparation. Easiest are encapsulated iron salts in plastic cartridge inserted directly into tree trunk, or use a foliar or soil applied iron chelate, or use iron salts with fertilizers in the soil.

Fertilizers lists

Precision Fertilizer Applications for Trees

While a general fertilizing with a balanced chemical fertilizer blend on a four to five year rotation suffices to keep trees healthy, there always is the gardener with a systematic approach who likes precision formulae. For these mathematically inclined tree lovers, here is a formula for calculating fertilizer applications.

The generally accepted rate of application of actual nitrogen for trees is one-half pound of nitrogen per inch of tree trunk diameter. This is predicated on applying a balanced formulation, usually a fertilizer with a Nitrogen:Phosphate:Potash ratio of 1:2:1 (as 5-10-5 fertilizer) or a ratio of 1:1:1 (as 10-10-10 fertilizer).

Divide the nitrogen number of the fertilizer into 100 to find the number of pounds of that particular material to make one actual pound of nitrogen. For example; the fertilizer is 5-10-5. $100 \div 5 = 20$. Twenty pounds of 5-10-5 fertilizer yields one pound of actual nitrogen.

Calculation Examples

The tree is 10 inches through at breast height, the fertilizer on hand is 20-20-20. $100 \div 20 = 5$ pounds of fertilizer to yield 1 pound of nitrogen. $5 \times (10 \times 1/2) = 25$ pounds of fertilizer to be distributed in holes drilled in the actively feeding root zone of the tree.

The tree is 30 inches in diameter, the fertilizer on hand is 5-10-5. $100 \div 5 = 20$ pounds of fertilizer to yield 1 pound of actual nitrogen. $20 \times (30 \times 1/2) = 300$ pounds of 5-10-5 fertilizer to be distributed among the holes drilled in the actively feeding root zone of the tree.

Fertilize trees only to keep them growing steadily at a moderate rate. Every three to five years usually is sufficient. If the tree is ailing, fertilize for two successive years, then wait three or more years.

Commercial liquid fertilizers for foliar fertilizing*

Trade name	% Nitrogen N	% Phosphoric Acid K	% Potash P
DuPont Foliar Fertilizer	19	22	16
Folium	20	20	20
Instant Vigoro	19	28	14
Orthogrow	10	5	5
Ra-Pid-Gro	23	21	17

*Never apply undiluted to plants but mix with water according to manufacturer's instructions and apply as directed on the label.

Organic materials useful as fertilizers

Animal product	Average % Nitrogen N	Average % Phosphoric Acid K	Average % Potash P	Speed of Availability
Dried Blood	12	0	0	moderate
Tankage	8 - 10	5 - 12	0	moderate
Steamed Bonemeal	1 - 2	22 - 30	0	slow
Bone Tankage	6	30	0	moderate
Fish Meal	8 - 10	5	0	moderate
Sheep Manure	2 - 3	1 - 2	1 - 2	slow
Poultry Manure	2 - 3	1	1 - 2	slow
Vegetable Product				
Cotton Seed Meal	8	2	2	slow
Hard Wood Ash	0	2	8	slow
Soft Wood Ash	0	2	4	slow
Linseed Meal	5	2	2	slow
Soybean Meal	6	3	1	slow

Manufactured fertilizer chemicals*

Chemical	Average % Nitrogen N	Average% Phosphoric Acid K	Average % Potash P	Speed of Availability	Reaction
Ammonium Chloride (*Muriate of Ammonium*)	26	26	0	quick	acid
Ammonium Sulfate	20	0	0	quick	very acid
Ammonium Nitrate	35	0	0	quick	acid
Sodium Nitrate (*Nitrate of Soda*)	16	0	0	very quick	alkaline
Potassium Chloride (*Muriate of Potash*)	0	0	50	quick	neutral
Potassium Phosphate	0	15	40	quick	neutral
Potassium Nitrate	12	0	40	quick	slightly acid
Rock Phosphate	0	25	0	slow	alkaline
Potassium Sulfate	0	0	50	quick	neutral
Superphosphate	0	20	0	slow	neutral
Mono-Ammonium Phosphate	12	60	0	quick	acid
Di-Ammonium Phosphate	20	53	0	quick	alkaline

*None of these is a complete fertilizer, supplying more or less balanced amounts of nitrogen, phosphate and potash. But they are useful where just one fertilizer element is lacking in the soil (in some cases, two), and for compounding fertilizer mixtures.

How to fertilize your tree

Trees, like other plants, depend on adequate mineral nutrition in the soil for healthy growth. While it is true that native trees growing in a forest situation get along with little added fertility but make do with what the soil has to offer, it is equally true that those same trees would be more vigorous with a faster growth rate and with handsomer foliage if they were supplied with additional fertilizer from time to time.

City trees, especially, need to be maintained in a vigorous, healthy condition to enable them to fend off detrimental factors in the environment. They suffer from air polution. Often city trees grow on fill soils or soils contaminated with various more or less toxic chemicals. Some city trees have to grow with roots restricted by pavements or buildings. In any community the trees receive only partial "full sunlight" due to atmospheric pollutants, and adding insult to injury, they cannot get a good night's rest because street or security lights prevent full darkness so necessary for full plant development. There is every reason to feed shade and ornamental trees in any situation, but city trees, especially, need ample fertilizer.

Three ways to fertilize

There are three basic ways of feeding trees. A fertilizer solution of specially formulated chemicals may be sprayed on the foliage and certain species are able to make optimum use of the nutrient chemicals. This is called foliar feeding. If your tree is one of those able to take up foliar fertilizer you can anticipate spectacular results. So far as photosynthesis and vital functions are concerned, the leaves are where the action occurs. When fertilizer is applied directly to the leaves and goes into the leaf cells, growth response is quick. Most nutrient elements enter trees through the roots. The other two ways of feeding trees have to do with supplying fertilizer to the root system. One way is to drill holes in the soil and to apply a dry fertilizer preparation. Gradually the fertilizer dissolves, filters out into the root zone, and the dissolved nutrient materials diffuse into the roots. The other way involves dissolving the nutrient preparation in water. The nutrient solution is pumped into the soil, and, again, nutrient chemicals diffuse into the roots.

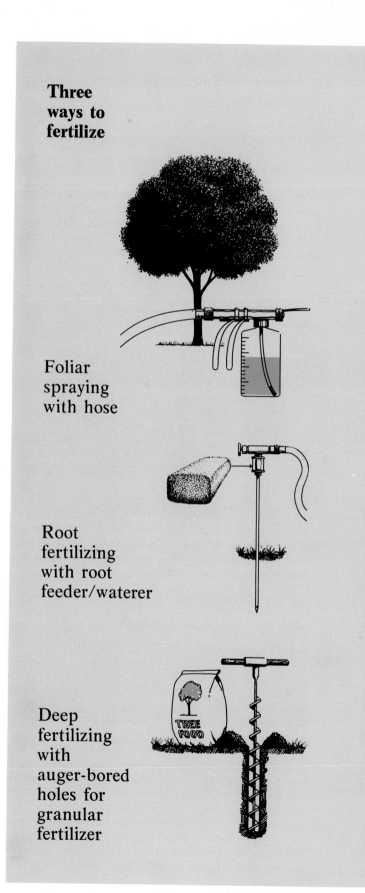

Three ways to fertilize

Foliar spraying with hose

Root fertilizing with root feeder/waterer

Deep fertilizing with auger-bored holes for granular fertilizer

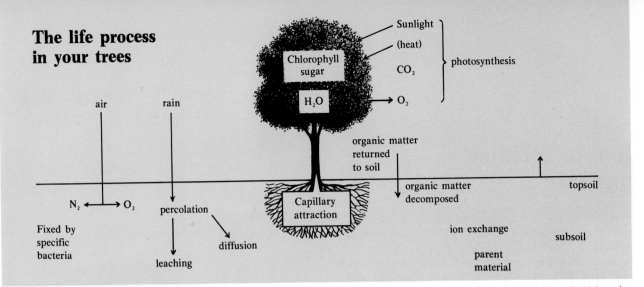

The life process in your trees

Sunlight
(heat)
CO_2 } photosynthesis

Chlorophyll sugar

H_2O → O_2

air   rain

organic matter returned to soil

organic matter decomposed   topsoil

N_2 ← → O_2 percolation   Capillary attraction   ion exchange   subsoil

Fixed by specific bacteria   diffusion   parent material

leaching

When sunlight shines on a green leaf, water (H_2O) and carbon-dioxide (CO_2) are combined in chlorophyll-bearing cells to make various carbohydrates, often simple glucose sugar. Carbon-dioxide must be able to diffuse inward for photosynthesis. Oxygen (O_2) is produced as a byproduct and escapes into the atmosphere. To allow for this exchange of gases, all cells inside the leaves are coated with a film of water. Thus, moisture is the single most important element in your tree's life process.

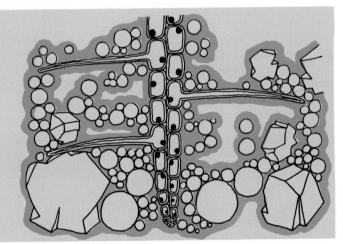

Soil solution (water containing dissolved minerals) diffuses from the spaces between soil particles into hair roots and then moves on into larger roots and thus up into the top of the plant.

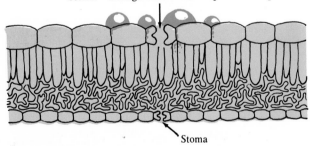

Stoma - through which water vapor and air pass

Stoma

A leaf cross-section showing how chlorophyll-bearing leaf cells function. Water diffuses from the vein to the cells, where photosynthesis occurs. Some water is lost as water seeps on through the stomata. Air diffuses into the leaf through the stomata and carbon-dioxide is utilized in photosynthesis. Oxygen produced by photosynthesis is partially used to support cell life, the excess diffuses out through the stomata.

Transpiration *is the loss of water vapor from leaves. Water coats all leaf cells and some evaporates into intercellular spaces and diffuses out of the leaf through the stomata.*

Respiration *is the break-down of a carbohydrate by a process of oxidation to release energy for life processes with carbon dioxide and water produced as waste products.*

How nutrients get into plants

Only liquids can enter plant cells. Dry fertilizer in dry soil is of no use at all to a plant. But when the soil becomes moist and the fertilizer dissolves, the dissolved nutrient elements carried in the soil water may diffuse into root cells. Large tree roots do not take up water or minerals. All intake is handled by tiny, delicate roots as small or smaller than a human hair. The larger roots we find in the garden are merely pipelines carrying absorbed water and minerals from the fine hair roots at the farthest extension of the roots to the trunk.

Foliar fertilizers function in the same manner. The fertilizer solution, when applied, hits the leaves and a very small amount of it enters leaves' breathing pores. Cells inside the leaves are coated with moisture and the fertilizer solution blends with the already present leaf liquids. Nutrients in the liquid coating the cells diffuse through cell membranes and are utilized by protoplasm in its vital functions.

The trunk of a tree (as well as the branches) is part of the pipeline system. All living tissues need water and minerals. Normally water and minerals enter through hair roots, are translocated through tubular tissues through the roots and up through the trunk and branches to the leaves where vital functions

JAN. | FEB. | MAR. | APR. | MAY | JUNE | JULY | AUG. | SEPT. | OCT. | NOV. | DEC.

**Fertilize
in spring**

**DO NOT
fertilize
in summer**

**Fertilize
in fall
after tree
is dormant**

occur. In the leaves carbohydrate substances are manufactured by photosynthesis and these food substances supply energy for all living cells in the plant. They are carried downward through the branches and tree trunk to the main roots and then to the secondary and hair roots to supply energy to the water and mineral absorbing cells. The minerals in fertilizers are not a source of energy. Rather, they make enzyme and hormone systems function so energy transfer can take place. The plant that is lacking in minerals cannot properly photosynthesize, respire, perform growth functions, or otherwise operate normally.

When is the best time to fertilize a tree?

Trees make their most vigorous growth after a resting period. In the North Temperate zone winter is the time of rest, vigorous growth occurs in the spring, and tapers off as summer wears on. In the subtropical climates of Zones 9 and 10 tree growth is intermittant. The plants grow a while, then rest a while. In these areas the need for year round fertility is important.

If you live where trees go dormant in winter schedule your fertilizing program to coincide with vigorous growth. Generally speaking, very early spring is an appropriate time to get fertilizer into the soil. By the time it is distributed through the soil solution that bathes the roots, root activity will be picking up, and the minerals will be transferred into the tree. Many experts recommend putting liquid or dry fertilizer into the soil as quickly as frost goes out of the ground in the spring. This is not a bad rule to follow.

Where soil is heavy, with a high clay fraction, late fall feeding is another option. After your tree is completely dormant and the soil is thoroughly cooled apply tree fertilizer solution or dry feed. The nutrient minerals will diffuse through the soil but will be held by the clay particles to be absorbed by the roots over winter and in early spring. Obviously, this is not a good practice for sandy or silt soils because much of the mineral material would leach downward beyond reach of the roots before spring root activity.

Avoid fertilizing trees after late spring. Summer feeding is risky business. It encourages continuous growth at a time when tissues need to harden off to be winter resistant. We notice a problem related to this on high quality cool weather grasses. People often fertilize cool weather grasses in late summer and in early fall to maintain a superior stand of grass. Some of this high nitrogen fertilizer diffuses down into the root zone of lawn trees and is taken into the roots. These nutrients stimulate renewed activity in the tree and sometime after a heavy frost various signs of injury appear. The bark pulls away from the wood because the succulent inner bark cells were ruptured by ice crystals. Tender, fall-produced twigs freeze back. Fall color is poor. All of these forms of injury may be caused by too much available fertilizer late in the growing season.

Foliar feeding is a handy way to perk up a weak tree in midsummer when root feeding may be risky. You can make up a solution of foliar fertilizer, spray it directly on the foliage to improve flagging growth, and the roots and trunk are not endangered. Because the leaves will fall with frost there is little danger to the top of the tree, either. A small amount of twig damage may appear if foliar feeding is carried out in the fall, but usually the damage is minimal. Midsummer foliar feeding is a handy technique for pushing young but well established trees in the garden.

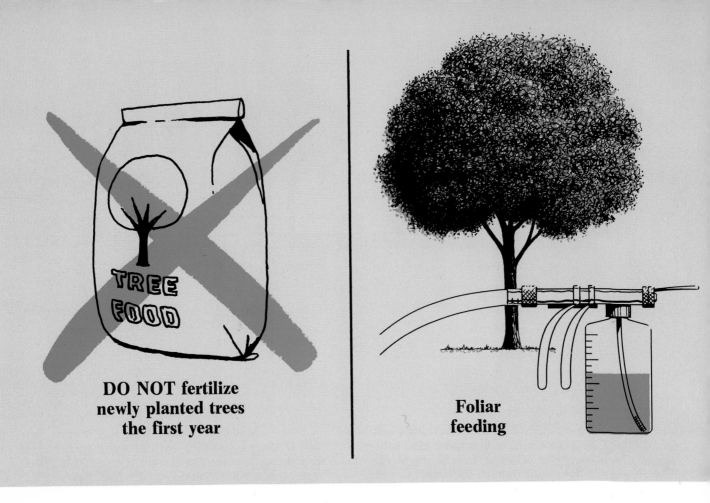

DO NOT fertilize newly planted trees the first year

Foliar feeding

A fertilizer program for newly planted trees

Do not fertilize newly planted trees the first year. You should have supplied a phosphate fertilizer when mixing the fill soil because ample phosphate is needed to encourage the early development of a vigorous root system. If you failed to apply phosphate at planting time, do it now with a hose attached tree fertilizing device (these sometimes are called root feeders) and cartridge-form fertilizer. Do not use general fertilizer cartridges; rather, use those intended for recently transplanted trees or the ones that supply only phosphate.

Whether your tree was planted in the fall or in the spring, you can begin to fertilize it the spring following its first summer in the garden. Again, the hose attached root feeder is a handy tool for the job. But you may apply dry fertilizer as described below. As soon as leaves appear you can apply a general foliar fertilizer. But do not overdo it this year. Remember, it takes several years for a tree to become fully established and you do not wish to crowd it into rapid growth until the roots are developed sufficiently to support a vigorously growing top. Early the third spring fertilize your new tree a little more generously. After that, add minerals to the soil to obtain the amount of annual growth you wish.

Foliar fertilizing technique

Foliar fertilizers are made up of special chemicals that can be absorbed by leaves and that, when properly applied, will not cause chemical damage (scorch) to leaves. To foliar feed your tree you need a quantity of foliar fertilizer and a pressure spray device.

Read the instructions on the fertilizer container. While it is all right to make up a solution more dilute than recommended (often this is desirable when the weather is hot) NEVER make up an over-strength solution because it will injure the foliage. Foliar feeding works best when leaves are tender and succulent, recently formed but full-sized and mature. Toward the end of summer most leaves develop a waxy layer that is impervious to fertilizer solutions. Late spring and early summer foliar feeding give the best results.

With at least some species, time of day makes some little difference. Very early (dawn) spraying seems to give the very best results, but so long as it is a bright day with little wind and a moderate temperature any time will do. Make up your fertilizer solution, set your sprayer for sufficient pressure to reach all parts of the tree with sufficient force to cause the leaves to move, and adjust the nozzle for

If you stake out a circle two or three feet beyond the dripline of the tree and another about one-third of the way from the trunk toward the outer circle, you will have defined a broad band in which almost all of the actively absorbing roots of the tree can be found.

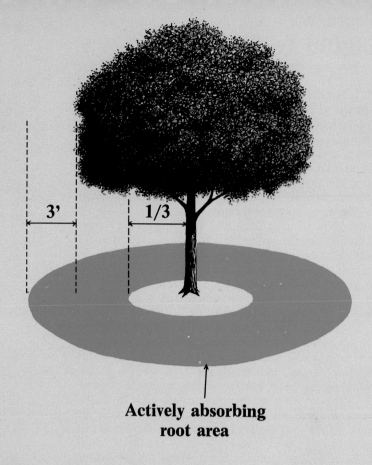

3' 1/3

Actively absorbing root area

the finest possible mist. Blow the mist through the tree, heavily coating under and upper surfaces of all leaves. Many garden pesticides and some fungicides are compatible with foliar fertilizers, so if you are spraying for insect or disease control you may wish to include foliar fertilizer in the control spray solution. Many rose growers do this with highly satisfactory results.

How much foliar fertilizer should you use? The instructions on the container will give specific recommendations for that particular formulation. Follow them exactly. In no case should you apply an overdose of foliar fertilizer because you might defoliate the tree.

Root fertilizing methods

The traditional method for fertilizing shade and ornamental trees is root feeding. Some specialists favor the wet method, others apply a fertilizer solution. Either technique gives first rate results if it is carried out properly.

The trick is to get the nutrient materials into the soil where actively absorbing roots are located.

Generally speaking, this is the area under the leafy portions of the horizontal branches. There is little reason to apply fertilizer close to the trunk of an established tree. Only large, conducting roots occur near the trunk; these do not absorb any appreciable amount of water or dissolved minerals. The greatest root activity takes place at about the dripline of the tree, that is, the outer reach of the branches. If you stake out a circle two or three feet beyond the dripline of the tree and another about one-third of the way from the trunk toward the outer circle you will have defined a broad band in which almost all of the actively absorbing roots of the tree can be found.

Tree roots seldom are as deep as inexperienced gardeners think. In a well maintained lawn most of the tree's root system may be within eighteen inches of the surface. Forest trees in some cases have more deeply penetrating roots because roots grow toward available nutrients and the forest floor may be largely exhausted. By nature, some trees develop roots just below the surface and these may, with time, actually become fully exposed. Many of the weedy sorts of trees fall in this category, but so do such desirable species as birches, horse-chestnuts, maples, and sweetgums. These can be encouraged to keep their roots down below the grass by applying fertilizer annually at ever-increasing depths.

As a rule of thumb, apply fertilizer solutions (liquid fertilizing) at a depth of fifteen to twenty-four inches. Bore holes to apply dry fertilizer to a depth of about eighteen inches.

Liquid fertilizing

This technique involves forcing a fertilizer solution into the soil in the area of actively absorbing roots. Commercial tree maintenance men dissolve special formulations of nutrient elements in large spray tanks, and pumping eighteen to twenty-two gallons per minute at three hundred pounds pressure they force the solution into the soil. Obviously, this high pressure method is beyond the average home owner.

The easy way for a home gardener to apply fertilizer in solution form to a tree is by using a hose attached tree root feeder. This tool consists of a perforated hollow rod that is shoved into the soil. At the top of the rod is a chamber into which a slowly dissolving fertilizer pellet (usually called a cartridge) fits. Above the fertilizer chamber there is a valve and beyond that the hose attachment.

To use the instrument insert a cartridge in the chamber, screw the tool onto the hose, insert the perforated rod into the soil to a depth of about eighteen inches, and gradually turn on the water. Handling the water pressure is important. Begin with the valve at the instrument turned off. Turn full water pressure into the hose, and very slowly open the valve on the root feeder. If you allow a full stream of water to develop too quickly chances are the fertilizer solution will be forced upward along the perforated rod to spill out over the surface of the ground. Slow and easy does it.

The perforations in the root feeder are along the sides near the lower end. These provide for a lateral (horizontal) flow of solution into the soil. If your soil is slightly damp results should be optimum. It is difficult to use a tree root feeder effectively when the soil is very wet or very dry. Follow instructions that come with the root feeder and with the fertilizer cartridges.

They will tell you how many cartridges to use for a tree of a specific size. To get an even distribution beneath the tree, use your best judgement. If your soil is heavy you should insert the feeder every twenty-four to thirty-six inches within that broad band defined to include most of the feeder roots. If your soil is more porous, three to six foot intervals may suffice.

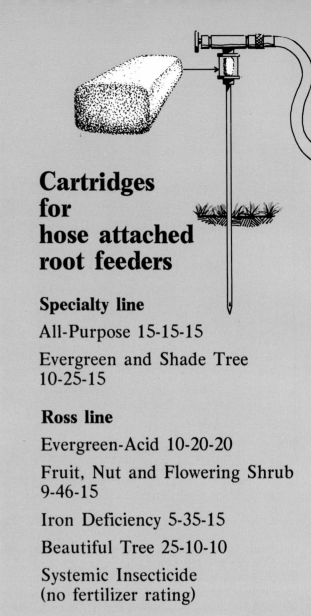

Cartridges for hose attached root feeders

Specialty line

All-Purpose 15-15-15

Evergreen and Shade Tree 10-25-15

Ross line

Evergreen-Acid 10-20-20

Fruit, Nut and Flowering Shrub 9-46-15

Iron Deficiency 5-35-15

Beautiful Tree 25-10-10

Systemic Insecticide (no fertilizer rating)

Dry fertilizing

Dry fertilizing offers the gardener a choice of fertilizer formulations which is a decided advantage. The disadvantage is the need for quite a large number of sizeable holes. Working within the area of actively absorbing roots as defined above, prepare holes on eighteen to twenty-four inch centers. The holes should be twelve to eighteen inches deep.

Several methods may be used to make holes for dry fertilizer. The best way is to drill them with a 1¾ inch or 2 inch diameter soil auger. Such a tool makes a clean hole without compressed sides and the soil from the hole comes out with the auger to be reserved for ultimately refilling the holes. A refinement of this method is to use a sod plugging tool to remove a plug of sod where each hole is to be drilled.

The plugs are replaced after fertilizer—usually topped with sand or a sand-soil mix—is in the hole. Another way to make holes is with water under pressure. Few homeowners would have a tool used professionally called a water lance. But your hose attached root feeder can be worked up and down to make a rather irregular hole with uncompacted sides. Such a hole takes fertilizer readily and the fertilizer quickly is absorbed into the soil because the sides of the hole are damp.

Never make holes with a crowbar or with a punchbar. Holes made by pounding a solid object into the soil have tightly compacted sides. Almost no fertilizer ever diffuses laterally from such a hole, and even vertical diffusion is greatly retarded. Punchbar feeding is relatively common in some parts of the United

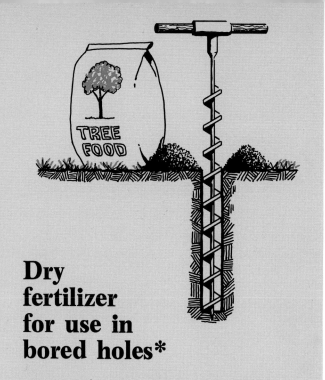

Dry fertilizer for use in bored holes*

Wumparo 14-14-14

Miller's Fertilizer 10-6-4

Vertagreen 10-8-6

Vertagreen 5-10-5

*Local manufacturers and farmers' cooperatives formulate fertilizer preparations similar to those listed below that are suitable for tree fertilizers. Often these are less expensive than general market fertilizers.

States; but it is a poor practice and should be discouraged.

The amount and formulation of fertilizer to apply to a particular tree varies with the species, with the vigor of the tree, and with soil conditions. Usually agricultural-type fertilizers rather than the light weight home lawn type fertilizers are used for trees. Common formulations are 10-6-4, 8-8-8, 10-10-10, and 5-10-5. These are available from dealers in agricultural chemicals, though most garden shops also carry a standard, heavy weight 5-10-5 formulated fertilizer.

For trees that measure six inches in diameter at breast height or less the usual recommendation is one to two pounds of fertilizer per one inch of trunk diameter. At the light rate, a five inch tree would take five pounds of fertilizer distributed in all the holes drilled in its root zone. At the heavy rate, the same tree would get ten pounds of fertilizer.

Trees that measure more than six inches in diameter at breast height are fertilized at rates varying between two and five pounds per inch of trunk diameter. Thus, an unthrifty ten inch tree in need of a good boost would get as much as fifty pounds of fertilizer distributed in the holes drilled in its actively feeding root zone.

The technique of completing a dry fertilizing program is as follows. Measure your tree's diameter at breast height (this usually is assumed to be four feet from the ground) to determine the amout of fertilizer you need. Following the instructions given above for locating the area of actively absorbing roots, with a soil auger drill twelve to eighteen inch-deep holes at eighteen to twenty-four inch intervals. Distribute the fertilizer as evenly as possible among the holes. Many experts mix as much as an equal volume (or more) of pulverized **dry** soil or dry sand with the fertilizer. This addition makes equal distribution easier, and it insures a residue to partially fill the holes when the fertilizer has dissolved away.

If sod plugs were removed, these are replaced after the fertilizer mixture is in the holes. Dry fertilizer is of no use to your tree. If it remains in dry soil for any length of time it will pick up traces of moisture and will set into virtually insoluble concretions. With the fertilizer in the holes, set a sprinkler under the tree and water the area thoroughly. Apply at least one inch of water. If there is no rain within three or four days, water thoroughly again. This triggers off diffusion of the fertilizer throughout the root zone of the tree and provides dissolved minerals for the roots.

Many experts feel that dry feeding is the least expensive way of adequately fertilizing a tree. They suggest that when choosing a fertilizer look for one with at least part of the nitrogen fraction in organic form. That is, in, say, a 10-6-4 blend, where the 10 indicates 10 pounds of nitrogen per hundred pounds, look for a label where the 10% nitrogen is not pure nitrate form. Rather, it could be ammonium nitrate, or urea, or ureaform. It could be a blend of, say, ammonium nitrate and urea. Calcium nitrate or a similar inorganic form is adequate. But urea, ureaform, or ammonium nitrogen gives better results in a tree fertilizing program.

Never overfertilize your trees. A fully established, quite young tree that needs to be pushed for the sake of design or for needed shade will take a light fertilizing every spring. A healthy, moderately sized tree needs to be fertilized only every third or fourth year, while the same tree in a puny state may need every other year feeding. Some judgement is needed here.

If the tree's problem has to do with a poor root system, apply a high phosphate fertilizer such as a 5-10-5 formulation and do not overdo it. If the roots are weak due to soggy soil make an effort to correct the drainage. A weak tree pushed into vigorous growth may react like a Roman candle—shoot right up, and soon die off. Fine, old mature trees in good condition benefit from every other year very light fertilizing. If the trees are weak generally—not due to deteriorated roots—a heavier fertilizing is indicated followed by lighter every-other-year applications. If there is no obvious need to fertilize a tree and you cannot decide whether to do it, give it a miss. Next year is soon enough.

CHAPTER 4
When and how to water your tree

Facts about plants and water

All living tissues require
a constant supply of water

When growing, plants need ample
water to supply new tissues

When in leaf, plants use large
amounts of water during light
hours for photosynthesis and
they lose water constantly through
leaf pores (transpiration)

While soil must contain
sufficient water to supply a
plant's needs for living
processes, for growth, for
photosynthesis, and for
respiration, the soil must never
remain soggy because roots
require oxygen

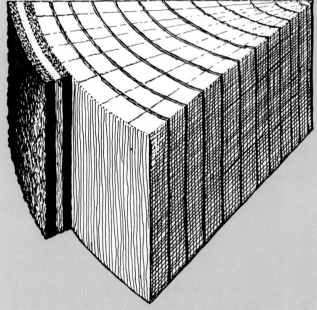

Are you familiar with the growth rings in a tree's
trunk? When you cut across a woody trunk or limb
and polish the surface you can see a series of
concentric rings. Each year as growth resumes in the
spring a new layer of wood is added just under the
bark. As there is plenty of moisture in the soil
following winter, and because minerals released by
frost activity are plentiful, and because the temperature is favorable, this first burst of growth is
composed of large cells.

But, as spring wears on into summer and the soil
dries out and temperatures rise, the cells get smaller
and smaller until, by midsummer, growth stops. The
difference in cell size accounts for visible rings in the
wood. In a wet year a wide ring is laid down. If the

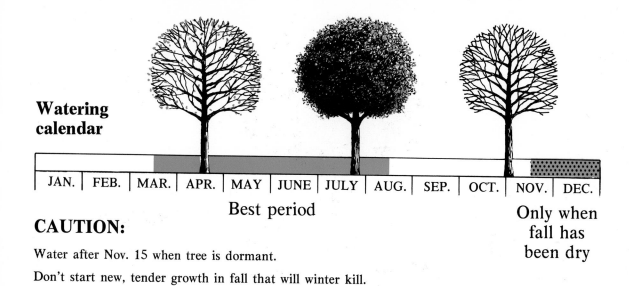

Watering calendar

JAN.	FEB.	MAR.	APR.	MAY	JUNE	JULY	AUG.	SEP.	OCT.	NOV.	DEC.

Best period

Only when
fall has
been dry

CAUTION:

Water after Nov. 15 when tree is dormant.

Don't start new, tender growth in fall that will winter kill.

winter and spring are dry, that year's growth ring is minimal. Some years an early summer drought stops growth but with late summer rains more cells are produced and then there are two rings for that year. The availability of water is of critical importance to tree growth. Trees will die from prolonged drought.

A tree needs ample water through summer not only for growth (and growth includes new twigs, leaves, and flowers as well as trunk diameter increase) but for vital processes. All living cells need water continuously, and as living processes speed up (activity is directly proportional to temperature) more water is needed. Then, in all green plants, there are two special processes that require large amounts of water. **(See illustrations showing how nutrients get into plants, Chapter 3, page 22.)**

Everybody knows about photosynthesis. Photosynthesis occurs only in living plant cells that contain the green pigment called chlorophyll. When light shines on a green leaf, chlorophyll bearing cells combine water and carbon-dioxide to manufacture various carbohydrates, often simple glucose sugar. No animals could survive very long without green plants, because they are the sole source of food energy. Photosynthesis (possible only in green plants) fixes solar energy and we eat the green plant or we eat its fruits or seeds.

Or we feed the plants to animals and eat the animals, but always, the original source of the energy that sustains animal life is from a green leaf. On a very warm summer day, a large tree utilizes several barrels of water for photosynthesis. When water is lacking in the soil, photosynthesis is retarded, and the tree suffers from the droughted condition.

Transpiration is the other process that takes great amounts of water. Leaves are furnished with tiny pores in their "skin" which allow an exchange of

gases—including oxygen, carbon-dioxide, and water vapor—from the atmosphere to the inside of the leaf. These pores, called stomata (one is a stoma = "little mouth"), are essential to the leaf. Carbon-dioxide must be able to diffuse inward for photosynthesis during light hours, and because a photosynthesizing cell produces oxygen as a byproduct, this excess oxygen must be able to escape.

All the cells inside the leaf are coated with a fine film of water and this water continuously evaporates into the spaces between the cells, and then some of it escapes through the pores of the leaves. On a hot, windy day, when leaves are waving around briskly in dry air, the water loss is unbelievable, amounting to hundreds of gallons in the case of some species of large trees such as sycamores. This transpirational loss calls for continually replaced water in the tree's system. The water has to come from the soil by way of the roots.

Now, we know why trees need plenty of water—water for cellular vital processes, for growth, for photosynthesis, and for transpiration. All of this water has to come from the soil. It enters the roots, diffusing into root hairs, moving through thin walled root tip cells, and then into the veins. It moves upwards in the veins into the most active wood (just under the bark) and into the leaves where the action is. Forests occur naturally where ample water occurs in the soil to supply the trees that grow there. But in artificial, garden situations, often we have to water our trees.

Several rules apply when watering trees. First, try to follow the normal pattern of rainfall, making up any deficiencies of the moment. Through most of the United States late winter and early spring are wet seasons. If the soil becomes unusually dry, trees have to be watered. Where leafy trees occur natively, late

Tree watering devices

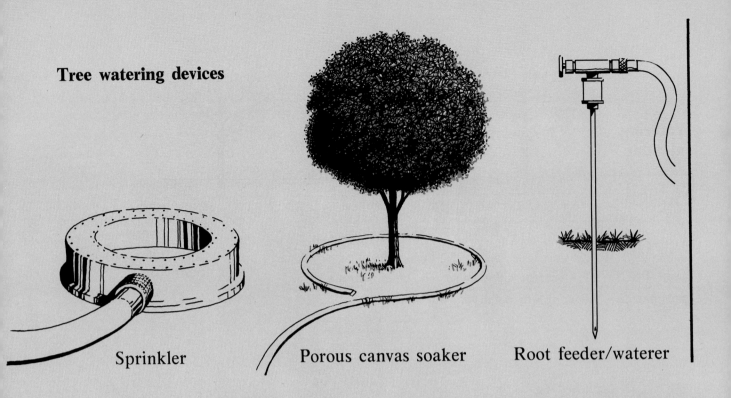

Sprinkler   Porous canvas soaker   Root feeder/waterer

spring and early summer rainfall generally averages about one to one and one-half inches per week. Later in the summer the rainfall dwindles to one inch or less per week. In the Prairie and Great Plains states summer rainfall is likely to be scanty. This is one of the factors that contributes to the normally treeless landscape. Because gardeners in these areas want trees for shelter, shade and for decorative purposes they have to modify the water supply, adding plenty of soil moisture through the summer months.

Keep your eye on the annual rainfall. If it is below average, week after week, make up the difference by watering your trees. How you do it is critical. Don't make a constantly soggy condition under any tree because tree roots have to have oxygen in order to survive. The best way is to apply a generous amount of water at one application, and then to let this move downward through the soil, pulling air in after it by capillary action. This will revitalize the root system of your trees.

Also, watch rainfall from a seasonal standpoint. If rainfall in your area has been deficient by Labor Day, water your trees thoroughly during September. The fall may turn off cold and wet in which case your efforts are largely wasted. On the other hand, the drought may carry right up through frosty weather. A tree that goes into winter in a dehydrated condition is in serious trouble. Yet, on the other hand in late fall before frost you can cause your tree to resume active growth if you water too late in the fall and this will make it susceptible to winter damage. Better water in late summer or very early fall if the soil is exceptionally dry.

When you water a tree, water deeply. Apply sufficient water so the soil is quite moist to a depth of at least one foot. Where the soil moisture is quite low and the soil is badly cracked or sunbaked you may have to water in two hitches. Set the sprinkler going for a few hours to soften the surface. Then wait twelve to twenty-four hours and water heavily so the water soaks way down to the root zone of the tree. If you live where watering is frequently required, by all means avoid frequent shallow applications because roots will grow upward toward the moist soil. Never water more frequently than once each week.

If sprinkling with a conventional lawn sprinkler seems inappropriate water your tree with a soil soaker or with a hose attached root feeder. The soil soaker is a porous canvas hose that attaches to your garden hose. Water slowly seeps from it and soaks downward into the soil. Little water is lost to evaporation or to wind movement with the canvas soil soaker but it takes practice to get uniform distribution of water with one of these and they work best only if the soil is nearly level. The root feeder, used with no fertilizer cartridge for plain watering, supplies water deep into the soil. People often make the mistake of pushing the root feeder too deep when watering with it in summer.

If the lateral holes in the shaft are twelve to fifteen inches below the surface water will spread throughout the root zone. Deeper water misses many of the active roots that absorb water. When placing the root feeder, shove the shaft vertically into the soil and then, without moving the instrument, turn on a very gentle flow of water. If you open the valve full force, chances are water will force its way up along the shaft of the root feeder and run off across the surface. You have to allow time for channels to open in the soil.

Newly planted trees should be watered about once each week when rainfall is less than one inch. Flood

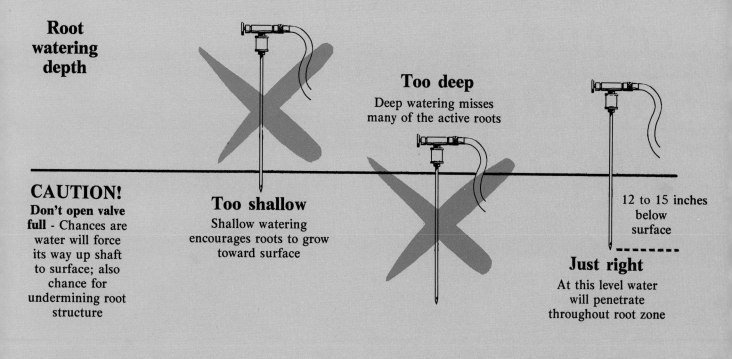

Root watering depth

CAUTION!
**Don't open valve
full** - Chances are
water will force
its way up shaft
to surface; also
chance for
undermining root
structure

Too shallow
Shallow watering
encourages roots to grow
toward surface

Too deep
Deep watering misses
many of the active roots

12 to 15 inches
below
surface

Just right
At this level water
will penetrate
throughout root zone

the tree's soil saucer once or twice, and then do not rewater until the soil is barely damp at the surface. A perpetually soggy condition prevents air from reaching tree roots and the airless condition will be fatal. Too wet soil will slow the establishment of your newly set tree. If the tree persists in wilting through the day even though the soil is moist, obviously the root system is incapable of taking in sufficient water to support the leafy top. Prune back sufficient new growth to ease the water demands. It really helps if you go out once or twice on hot, windy days and with the hose nozzle adjusted to a very fine mist thoroughly syringe the foliage of newly planted trees. This cools them and retards transpiration loss of water vapor.

Trees that have been planted for just a few years, say less than five years, need to be watered deeply when rainfall is scanty for two or three weeks. These trees probably do not have sufficient roots to supply water to the leafy crown when soil moisture is low. Therefore, you have to make up the difference. With the sprinkler, soil soaker, or root feeder (irrigator), water the tree thoroughly, then wait two or three weeks before rewatering. Recently planted trees, being scarcely established, may suffer serious setbacks if allowed to suffer for lack of water.

Older trees usually can go through all but the worst droughts with little or no extra water, but they are not the better for having to go waterless through any drought. Try to water every older tree on the property at least once each month during a drought. Because watering sometimes is banned in some communities during drought periods, you need to know about other steps that may possibly save your desiccated tree. One reasonable approach is to prune over the leafy crown of the tree, cutting away the

water consuming foliage. You can remove as much as one-third of the top growth of a tree during a drought period to reduce photosynthesis and transpiration demands for water. It seems sad to have to do this, but better severe surgery than the loss of the tree.

On rare occasions, winter watering becomes necessary. This is more critical with needle and with broadleaf evergreen species, but even some deciduous trees may suffer if subjected to a two or three month waterless winter period. When the soil is not frozen, apply sufficient water to penetrate to the root zone. Winter watering is far more successful when done with a hose attached feeder because the cold surface soil sometimes retards the intake rate. Also, sprinkling is likely to wake up the grass or ground cover plants which then will be injured by subsequent cold periods.

Mulching is a recognized method of preventing water loss from soil due to drying at the surface. While this technique has little application under established shade and ornamental trees, it certainly has its place where newly planted trees are concerned. If you have a problem with maintaining reasonable soil moisture at the root zone of a newly planted tree, by all means fill the watering saucer with a loose mulch of straw or hay. Not only will this mulching material keep the sun and air from drying the soil too rapidly, the shade cast by the mulch will provide a cooler root run, thus encouraging faster root development. The mulch in the watering saucer will somewhat complicate watering. You may have to fill the saucer two or three times to thoroughly soak the soil to a depth of a foot or more, but because you will not have to return to do the job over again for ten days or two weeks, you have still gained on the project.

31

CHAPTER 5
How to prune your tree

How to clean pruning tools

Immediately after use wipe off all plant gum and dried sap with an alcohol soaked rag.

Rub blades and all metal parts with an oil-soaked rag.

Squirt light machine oil on joints and articulated sections.

If rust spots develop

Spread on "liquid wrench" or transmission fluid.

After 20 minutes, rub lightly with very fine steel wool until metal is clean.

Apply warm machine oil, rub thoroughly.

Terms that apply to pruning

Callus—New tissue originating from the cambium layer (just under the bark) that will cover over a wound or a cut.

Cambium—A cylinder of tissue separating the bark and wood that is responsible for the annual increase in girth of a tree. It produces new wood cells and new bark cells.

Cut—Exposed wood that shows after a branch has been removed.

Cut-back—Reduction in the total top growth of a tree.

Dormant—A state of no active growth, as during the winter months.

Drop-pruning—The removal of a branch at a crotch. When a tree is to be thinned (cut-back) drop-pruning is the only acceptable method of taking branches from the leafy crown.

Girdling Roots—Roots growing closely round the trunk of a tree just above or below the ground. These roots eventually will strangle the tree.

Healing—Occurs when callus tissue covers a cut.

Precut—The removal of a branch at least six inches from the parent stem as a safety precaution to avoid bark tear-down. Following the precut the stub is removed.

Scar—Natural or man-made lesions penetrating the bark of a tree so the wood is exposed.

Sucker—Vigorously growing abnormally placed shoots that break from main branches, trunk or even from roots.

Tear-down—Occurs when a large branch is cut close to the parent trunk or limb; as the cut weakens the wood, the branch sags, ripping away bark and wood to create a nasty wound that is difficult to repair and slow to heal. A precut will prevent a tear-down.

Thinning—The removal of live branches by drop-pruning to create more space in the crown of a tree.

Topping—Stubbing back main limbs. This is a horticulturally unacceptable technique because it creates ugly trees and invites insect infestations and disease.

Tracing—Cutting away the bark from the edges of a wound following the sap flow pattern. This encourages rapid callus production and results in early healing of a wound.

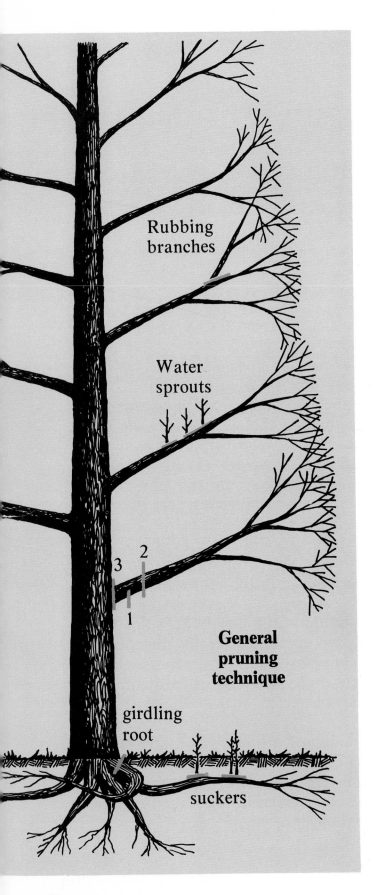

Rubbing
branches

Water
sprouts

3 2

1

**General
pruning
technique**

girdling
root

suckers

How to prune your tree

We prune plants to get more out of them. Proper pruning will give you a tree of better form, especially when pruning begins while the tree still is quite young. Pruning makes trees more attractive; an ornamental maple tree can be pruned to emphasize the gnarled beauty of its branches, birches can be pruned to expose their handsome trunks, shade trees can be pruned to develop elegant leafy crowns that provide pleasing shelter while resisting wind damage. This sort of pruning is called maintenance pruning. From time to time you can take your pruning tools and work over a tree or two, balancing and directing its growth to make it a greater asset to the garden.

The time to prune

Most trees can be pruned almost any time of the year. But the season of pruning makes a difference in subsequent growth of the tree. Some trees should be pruned just after seasonal growth ends as they are "bleeders", that is, unusual amounts of sap drain from pruning wounds, weakening the tree and preventing wounds from healing properly. Among the bleeders are walnuts, most birches, and the maples. Prune these in midsummer for best results.

Winter versus summer pruning

Summer pruning tends to limit post-pruning growth. Winter pruning often results in a vigorous burst of growth the following spring. American orchard keepers in early days developed the technique of pruning in winter because winter was a slack time (most orchards operated as a segment of a general farm) and many gardeners have picked up the practice of pruning in winter. There is something to be said for pruning a leafless tree—you can see the framework of branches (technically known as the scaffold) and can remove branches uniformly. But this benefit is more than offset by disadvantages.

If your tree is in normal health and you prune it in winter, you can count on very vigorous recovery growth the following spring. New shoots will be overlong. Watersprouts may spring up along the branches and even from shallow roots. The leafy load that you had hoped to lighten turns out to become heavier than ever. Winter pruning is a handy way to rejuvenate a decrepit old tree.

Each winter over three or four years take out one or two unneeded major limbs, cutting them right back to the trunk or point of origin, and drop-prune here and there in the crown to even out the scaffold of branches. Follow up with early summer pruning to shorten the leafy shoots just a little. Such pruning, coupled with a fertilizing program, can restore vigor to a tired old tree in just a few years.

It is interesting to look at the reasons for growth responses to winter and summer pruning. A deciduous (leaf-losing) tree is dormant in winter; next year's growths already are formed in miniature in the buds. All it takes is warm weather, moisture, and nutrients to trigger growth. The number of buds set the previous summer are more or less equated to the strength of the root system. When winter pruning removes a substantial number of those buds, the spring vigor will be distributed among the remaining buds. This is the main reason for overly vigorous growth in spring following winter pruning.

You see, as the weather breaks in spring, generally the soil moisture is high; mineral nutrients are plentiful having been released into the soil by frost action. Everything is there for a fine burst of growth. There are as many roots as before, but less "top." The result is overgrowth of active buds, and the initiation into activity of buds that normally would have remained dormant. These latent buds usually operate as standby organs, to break into growth only when catastrophe strikes. But winter pruning resembles catastrophe, and ample water and nutrition join in to trigger these latent buds into growth. From them come the watersprouts on the trunk, main limbs, and even, in some cases, from roots.

On the other hand, by early summer the soil has more or less dried out and available minerals have been absorbed by vigorous spring root activity. The weather is getting hot. Tree growth slows and finally stops—energy is spent. Now the tree will utilize what soil water is available for photosynthesis in the leaves. Energy-yielding carbohydrates produced by foliar photosynthesis will feed the "tired" twigs, branches, trunk and roots, and some will be used to make buds for next year's growth.

Then here you come along and scientifically prune over the top of the tree, doing all those necessary chores, and in doing them, remove leaf-bearing branches. There go the factories that were making food for the tree! The roots will be less vigorous now, and right through next spring. Fewer buds will form. Almost surely, insufficient soil moisture and minerals are available to make new leafy shoots even if the weather were more favorable. No wonder summer pruning represses growth for a season or two! By all means, prune as much as possible in the summer so the job lasts.

Summer pruning for ornamental trees

Summer pruning is an ideal method for developing vigorous ornamental and shade trees, maintaining them with a minimum of overgrowth. Several techniques are involved.

Pinching is the first of these. While it scarcely is feasible to pinch over the top growth of a fine old shade tree, it certainly is possible to pinch the new shoots of a broomstick-sized sapling or a small ornamental specimen. This is an important point. Remove growth while it is as young as possible, and the tree suffers a minimum from the operation. It is practical, too. The next time you have to saw off a four-inch diameter limb and worry about disposal after the job of cutting off the limb, think how nice it would have been if you had nipped off that badly placed limb when it was a slender switch with half a dozen leaves. Look at your young trees carefully as the new growth expands. Is a shoot overly vigorous, unbalancing the form of your tree? Pinch it back just beyond a leaf. Are far too many succulent little leafy shoots breaking out of the trunk?

Remember, each of these will become a big limb some day so they should be spaced. Rub off the extra ones while they are succulent and tender. If the tree has been planted within the past two or three years, better nip back all new growth by one-third or so, to keep the top proportionate to the not quite reestablished root system. Pinching new shoots is a profitable pastime.

Thinning young and old trees is a worthwhile thing to do. Not every tree needs to be thinned, and one properly thinned should not need rethinning for several years. Thinning consists of taking out a portion of the leafy crown of the tree, preferably without disturbing the general silhouette. In a dense, native stand, branches are crowded together and some get shaded out, to die and fall. An ornamental tree in the open garden is not subjected to this natural "pruning" process. There are particular steps to proper thinning.

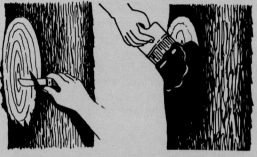

To remove a limb make clean, smooth cuts and leave no stubs to invite decay or infection. Figure at left shows the proper cut (A) to eliminate a crotch which may result in future injury. To remove a lateral limb (Figure at right), cut parallel to the main trunk or parent limb. Limbs of considerable weight should be undercut (A) and top cut (B) before the parallel cut (C) is made. This prevents splitting and stripping bark from the tree.

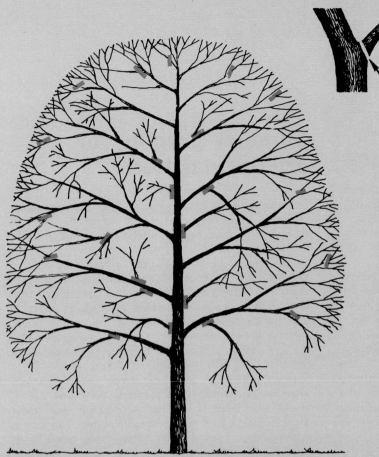

Drop pruning

Structure guides pruning. This typical tree is drop-pruned as shown, to control spread and to lighten the load at the ends of the branches. Crossing and weak branches are removed where they originate at the trunk.

For facing and sealing a wound, with a drawknife or chisel work the face of the wound until it is smooth and even. Next, with your drawknife or a heavy pocket knife work around the margin of the wound, making a uniform bevel, about 45°, where the bark joins the wood. With all disease-catching snags and irregularities removed, you are ready to seal the wound. Apply tree wound dressing. This may be a sort of paste-like paint or an aerosol tree wound dressing.

Drop pruning

Placement of cuts is of prime importance. **ALWAYS** cut at a crotch or where a branch originates. **NEVER** cut a branch off leaving a stub. Take a look at how a tree branch grows. It is composed of a series of Y's (this is called dichotomous branching). If a branch leaving the trunk makes a Y and each of the two new branches make Y's, and this goes on twice more the twigs at the end of that limb should add up to sixteen.

If we begin out at the twigs and take off one of each pair, we lighten the leafy load of the tree by fifty percent. This is very heavy pruning, and usually we do not do it that way. We look at the overly dense areas and prune away a branch or two, perhaps cutting back to the third, fourth, or fifth crotch from the tip. A nearby cut never is made at the same level, but is made deeper into the tree or closer to the leafy crown. Always dropping back to a crotch to make a cut is called drop-pruning. It is **the** way to make cuts in the leafy crown of a tree.

Sometimes a large limb appears to be unnecessary. It rams its way up through other branches, crowding and rubbing them. Or it is too low and needs to be removed so the car can get into the garage, or its presence throws the tree out of balance. It has to go. There are problems with large limb removal.

Wood is heavy stuff. A sizeable limb weighs several hundred pounds and you are planning to sever its support. Be sure that weight does not fall on you. A limb represents quite a balancing act. Most of its weight is concentrated far beyond the point of attachment. When you make a cut and upset the balance, that limb is going to swing. Position yourself so you do not get involved in the movement of the falling limb.

The place to cut a major limb is as close to the trunk of the tree (or to the larger branch from which it originates) as possible. But not right away. You **have** to get rid of all that unbalanced weight.

Place your ladder—or stand with your pole saw—

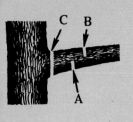

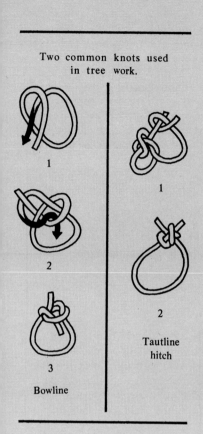

Two common knots used
in tree work.

1

2

3
Bowline

1

2
Tautline
hitch

When Removing a Large Limb—Tie your ladder to the base of the limb you will cut. You are going to drop the limb, leaving a stub attached to the tree. Then, you are going to do fine surgery in removing the stub. So, you must take precautions by securing your ladder because the falling branch or stub could head directly toward the legs of your ladder and knock it out from under you. It is dangerous to fall, more so with a saw.

When Removing the Butt or Stub—After the bulk of the limb has been removed, move your ladder and secure it to the trunk of the tree and position it so you can readily address and cut the remaining butt or stub. If the butt or stub remaining is a heavy one, toss the rope over a higher limb, and snub it to a nearby tree so the weight of the stub is supported by the rope, thus providing less interference with your sawing.

Ladder work safety rules

**Make certain ladder legs
are level, properly inclined
and tied to limb or trunk**

near the trunk so you can make a cut one to two feet out on the limb. Tie your ladder to the limb base. You are going to drop the limb leaving a stub attached to the tree. Then you are going to do a surgical job of taking off that stub. To drop the limb, saw from beneath to make a cut one-fourth to one-third of the way through the branch.

Then place your saw above the lower cut and saw straight downward. The branch will sag and probably it will break away before your saw cuts meet. Watch that falling butt—it may head right for the legs of your ladder. That's why the ladder is tied to the base of the limb. It is awkward to have a ladder knocked from under you, and dangerous to fall at all, more so to fall with a saw.

With the bulk of the limb removed, move your ladder to the trunk of the tree and position yourself to cut off the branch stub. If the stub is a heavy one, better tie a rope around it, toss the rope over a higher limb, and snub it to a nearby tree or bush so the weight of the stub is supported by the rope and will not interfere with neat saw work. As before, make an undercut, but this time take care to parallel the trunk

of the tree. Make your overcut with equal care. When the stub is down, your next job is facing and sealing the wound.

With a drawknife or chisel work the face of the wound until it is smooth and even. Next, with your drawknife or a heavy pocket knife work around the margin of the wound, making a uniform bevel, about 45°, where the bark joins the wood. The callous tissue to seal the cut surface will emerge from the bark-wood interface so it is important that this critical area be neatly trimmed to healthy tissue. With all disease-catching snags and irregularities removed, you are ready to seal the wound.

Apply tree wound dressing. This may be a sort of paste-like paint or an aerosol tree wound dressing. Spread or spray the black, rubbery material uniformly over the cut. Apply several very light layers rather than one heavy one. Even so, if the cut was a large one, you will have to come back two or three times to replace the protective coating as it weathers away. Eventually callous tissue will entirely cover the wound, bark will develop, and no evidence will show to mark the trunk.

Tools for pruning

The home garden pruning tool chest need not be extensive. But quality is important. Pruning is heavy work in most cases; even with the best of tools considerable judgement is needed to know which tool to use. More secateurs (hand pruners) are lost to overlarge branches than to anything else. More good loppers are hopelessly sprung cutting too-large branches than are lost to any other misuse. Know the limitations of your tools, and select the right tool for the job accordingly.

Here are the tools that make up a good home pruning kit:

Tree wound dressings

It is worth going into more detail about tree wound dressing. The purpose of this material is to exclude disease organisms and insects, and to protect exposed wood from weathering. One good rule is always to treat all woody cuts that expose an area larger than a nickle. Needless to say, cuts should be sealed while quite fresh. If a wound has weathered, whittle back to fresh wood and then apply the dressing. In some parts of the country it is fashionable to substitute various kinds of household paint for tree wound dressing. In the days of fine lead paints made up with linseed oil and turpentine such a practice was permissible—though no such paint ever duplicates a good, rubber-base, disease inhibitor-containing wound dressing—but modern paints, with their caustic solvents and strange pigments often are extremely toxic to plants. Avoid applying household paints to plants.

Suckers and Watersprouts. For any of several reasons very vigorous whippy, unbranched shoots may develop from tree trunks, main branches, and even from roots out in the lawn. These things, when on the tree trunk or main branches, are called watersprouts. Sprouts from roots are called suckers. Watersprouts and suckers come from dormant, microscopic buds buried in the tissue beneath the bark. The buds break into active growth when stimulated by heavy pruning, particularly winter pruning, or when the plant is injured or in poor health.

Never allow watersprouts or suckers to become woody. If you can catch them when they are just emerging, rub them away with a gloved hand (pull suckers when soil is wet). If they develop any size, with a curved wood gouge dig out a small cup of woody tissue from their point of origin and carefully plug the wound with grafting wax or tree putty, and then seal with tree wound dressing. One of the best ways to destroy suckers is to dig down in midsummer to their origin. Prune away the sprout-producing root.

Secateurs. This is the hand pruner we use most. It comes in one of two basic designs. Either the tool has a scissors action, that is, one cutting blade **passing** another, or it has blade and anvil action, that is, a blade cuts squarely against an "anvil" of solid, soft metal such as brass. There are good and bad points to both sorts.

An inexpensive pruner is a cheap tool. Usually the same poor metal is used to make the blade (which ought to be fine tool steel) and the handle. Or, if the blade is a different piece of metal the quality still is poor, the blade is fastened with cheap hollow rivets that soon loosen, and hinges, springs, and clasps are of equally poor quality material and design. The best quality pruners have cast or forged handles, carefully hand-finished down to a sturdy, comfortable grip. The blades, expertly forged, are screwed or hot-riveted into place. The hinge is adjustable, the spring is of spring steel and is replaceable, and the clasp that holds the tool shut fits and holds. Such a tool needs care. After each use, wipe it with a rubbing alcohol-soaked rag and then with a rag barely moistened with fine oil. Place a drop or two of oil at the hinge and at the clasp joint if it is exposed. Wrap the tool in a piece of duck or slip it into a leather pouch. If your are not one to care for good tools, do not invest in a good quality pruner. Rather, buy a reasonably made cheap one at the beginning of each season and discard it in the fall. Do not carry it over and use it, sprung and weak, to make ragged, destructive cuts on your plants.

Two or three pairs of secateurs make gardening easier. There is the small, razor sharp one for delicate new growth and soft stems. There is the middle-sized one for pruning over year-old growth and similar light wood. Then there is the large, heavy one for cutting wood up to half-inch in diameter. Here is a good rule of thumb; if the branch to cut will not enter two-thirds of the way between the blades of the tool, go to a larger tool as the one at hand is too small for the job.

Loppers. This tool comes in many styles. The basic model consists of a pair of heavy, curved scissor-type blades mounted on eighteen to thirty-inch long handles. This is the tool to reach for when the branch does not slide well into the blades of the hand pruner. Most of us do not use the lopper often enough and our hand pruners suffer for it. Leverage makes the small blades of the lopper workable. If the metal extensions of the cutting blades are too light they will collapse when you apply strong pressure to the handles. If the handles are of hollow aluminum they will collapse when you apply strong pressure. If the handles are of poorly grained wood or if good wooden handles have been abused, wooden handles will split under pressure. Some of the best loppers consist of tool steel cutting blades held by very heavy iron mountings that attach to iron handles with wood or metal grips. A good feature is a shock absorbing devise between the handles just back from the blades. This protects your wrists and forearms when a heavy limb suddenly yields and is cut through with a jolt.

Loppers come in various sizes and a modestly proportioned one with direct action (as contrasted to very heavy duty commercial models with a double-leverage action) suffices for most home needs. The well-into-it gardener may wish to keep an eighteen inch-long lopper for handy, light work and a more massive twenty to thirty-inch tool for heavier work. The lopper is used to cut branches larger than one-half inch, up to not more than one and one-fourth inches in diameter. Beyond that, a saw is needed. Loopers, like secateurs, need high maintenance. After use, wipe the blades with alcohol to remove tree gum and sap, then go over all metal parts with an oily rag.

Saws. Tree saws are a special breed. The teeth are coarse and often they are alternately twisted slightly. Such an arrangement makes a fairly wide groove, cutting coarse sawdust which falls free rather than clogging. For work around home two saws do the job. One needs to be of small size, say, a twelve or fourteen inch-long blade, tapering to a point. This little saw permits cutting in tight crotches and other narrow places. The larger saw, sixteen to twenty-two inches, cuts larger branches. If you care for your tools, buy good saws as the best ones not only are made of top grade metal, but the teeth are properly formed, properly sharpened, and with a special "set", that is, twist, for most efficient cutting. Cheap saws need to be replaced frequently—they are scarcely worth having sharpened as they do not hold an edge well. Saws may be straight or curved. Experts almost always use the curved saws as they give the most cutting action with the least arm movement. Ama-

teurs find these easy to use, too. You may find at least the smaller sized saws in folding models; the blade folds into a slot in the wooden handle pocket knife fashion. Such a saw is handy to have, but use it properly and by all means lock the blade into place before cutting or it will fold at the wrong moment and your knuckles will be lacerated, caught between jagged saw teeth and the saw handle. Occasionally straight bladed saws with teeth on both sides of the blade (coarse and fine) are offered. These, too, often booby-trap the inexperienced user.

Hedge shears. The hedge shears is meant for shearing hedges; amateurs attempt to use this tool for everything from digging dandelions to pruning the evergreens and shaping ornamental trees. While you need a hedge shears if your garden features clipped hedges, restrict the use of the tool to that garden feature. Never use a shears for general pruning.

Pole pruners and saws. One of the handiest things a home gardener can own is a set of pole pruning equipment. This includes a pole pruner with a cutting head somewhat similar to a lopper, and a pole saw. The tools mount on long poles; you stand on the ground and work as high as ten or fifteen feet in the air with these. The trouble is, pole pruners and saws meant for home use are flimsy, worthless gadgets in most cases. If your garden shop does not carry professional quality equipment ask your nurseryman or commercial tree care man to buy good ones for you. Use these just as you would the short-handled versions.

Ladders. Every gardener who plans to do some or all of his own pruning needs at least two ladders. Both can be household ladders also used for painting, gutter work and the like. One should be a very sturdy step ladder. The other should be an extension ladder. When you are pruning often you are reaching way out. You and the ladder are apt to come crashing down unless the ladder is on level footing and, preferably, secured at the top. Never work from an extension ladder resting free against a limb or the trunk of a tree. Your first job on climbing the ladder is to tie the top of both side rails to the tree. If your ladder is a light weight sort—aluminum or magnesium alloy—make up several sausage-shaped sand bags and drape these over the lowest rung of the ladder for added stability. Falling from a ladder is unpleasant, at best. Falling with a cutting tool in hand can cost you an eye or worse. **Never** use a metal ladder in a tree through which power lines run.

Ropes. Every home pruning buff needs a few lengths of rope. For tieing your ladder to the tree; for temporarily bundling brush, and so on. From the garden shop or hardware store buy some ten foot lengths of sturdy white cotton rope, something about twice the thickness of ordinary clothesline. For lowering heavy limbs, tools, and so on from the tree, buy a length or two of five-eighths inch hemp rope—usually a forty or fifty foot piece is more than sufficient. Rope requires good care. After use wipe it with a clean rag, coil it loosely, and hang the coil in a cool, dry place. If your rope gets wet, dry it as quickly as possible without overheating it. Friction or adhesive tape wrapped round the ends will keep the rope from frazzling.

Tree wound dressings. Tree wound dressings may be paste or paint-like. The good ones are based on a rubber emulsion and usually contain an asphalt fraction of some sort and a fungus sur-pressing chemical. Apply the thick pastes with a putty knife, working the material back and forth across the cut surface to fill all interstices and scrape off excess dressing to leave a uniform, thin layer. Apply paint-type dressings with a brush, brushing out the dressing for good penetration and a thin, even coating. For the home-owner the aerosol preparations are easiest. Shake the container well **at warm room temperature** and spray from a foot or more from the wound. Apply two or three very thin layers for best results.

Power pruning tools. Fortunately few homeowners seem to invest in power saws, power pole pruners and similar tools. Experts rely on these tools to do their job efficiently and quickly. But for the homeowner, scarcely used to climbing a tree or a ladder, and scarcely adept with power pruning equipment, these things can be lethal. Rely on good quality hand pruning equipment; if the job is extensive enough to require power tools, send for an expert.

Tool maintenance. Keep your pruning tools in a clean, dry place. After each use wipe the cutting parts with alcohol to remove dried gum and sap and then wipe all metal with an oily rag. Sharpening curved secateurs, lopper, and pole pruner blades as well as pruning saws is beyond the amateur. These are jobs for the experts. If yours is a good tool, worth spending money on, send it to a local cutlery specialist for sharpening—this is a good job for January. If your tools are inexpensive, use them until they no longer make clean cuts and then replace them with new ones.

For pruning special trees in special situations, see chapter 7, page 48.

Secateur or scissor-action clipper—Most frequently used hand pruner. Best quality have cast or forged handles. Forged blades are fastened with an adjustable screw. Spring is spring grade steel and is replaceable.

Needle-nosed secateur—This small, needle-nose hand pruner is kept razor sharp for removing delicate new growth and soft stems.

Anvil-clipper—This pruner's single cutting blade strikes on an anvil of solid, soft metal, such as brass. An advantage of the anvil clipper is that the design prevents lodging of twigs or branches between blades.

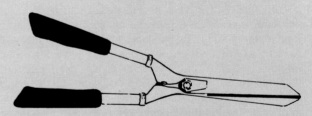

Hedge shears with serrated blades—The hedge shears with serrated blade and limb notch is used mainly for shearing hedges. Best models have shock absorbing grips of rubber or similar resilient material. Best blades are drop-forged and hollow-ground. This is a special pruning tool.

Pruning knife—The pruning knife is useful for smoothing a cut face after sawing. It is a useful but tricky tool for cutting back summer growth on trees, shrubs and roses. Properly used, with a 45° cut just above a leaf, it will do less damage than a pruner and you can work faster.

Guide to pruning tools

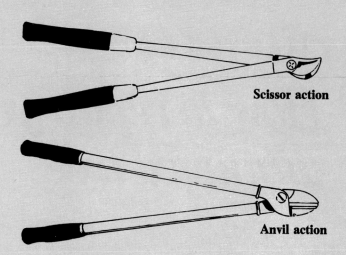

Scissor action

Anvil action

Lopping shears—Lopping shears are 2-hand pruners for heavy-duty work. As with the secateurs models are offered in the scissor-action or anvil-action type. The soft-metal anvil is adjustable and replaceable. Lopping shears are available in a variety of lengths and with handles of a variety of materials including wood, tubular steel and aluminum, though the latter is not too durable.

Folding saw—This light-weight, compact tool is excellent for tight angles, close work and small jobs. You'll need a heavy-duty unit in your tool shed for many pruning jobs.

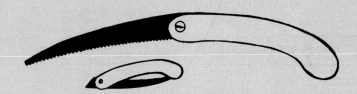

Main pruning saw—This type with high quality steel blade, regular but coarse teeth, and a slightly curved blade is your most reliable all around pruning saw. It should be the main pruning saw in your tool shed.

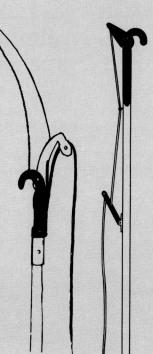

Pole pruner and saw—Extension pole pruners are essential tools if you have shade trees. The lever-action hook removes branches up to slightly more than an inch in diameter. For larger limbs, you can use the detachable saw available with many models. Wood or fiberglass poles are recommended if you have electrical power lines overhead near your trees. The detachable saws are similar in design to rigid handle curved pruning saws and usually cut on the pull stroke.

Speed saw—raked teeth—This type of saw is best for fast rough cutting. It can handle 3 in. and bigger limbs, and green wood without jamming. It is an economical, safe substitute for the small power saw jobs. But, you'll have to draw knife smooth the roughed cutting face it leaves.

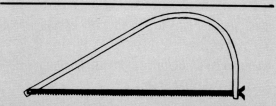

Bow saw—The bow saw, although frequently used for general pruning and limb removal, is designed for "bucking" or firewood cutting. It is difficult to use in branchy trees.

CHAPTER 6

How to repair your damaged tree

Five general rules

1. Immediately trim away all splintered, lacerated wood and bark. Rough surfaces provide perfect breeding places for decay fungi.

2. Bevel injured bark, tracing it back to firmly attached, unharmed tissue. Callus tissue will regrow much more quickly from below properly trimmed bark, and callus tissue will heal the wound.

3. Where branches are damaged and must be removed, always cut at a crotch (drop prune). Never leave a stub.

4. If possible, maintain the natural form of the tree while pruning—not always too easy. Sometimes it helps to prune uninjured wood to maintain tree configuration.

5. Apply tree wound dressing to any cut or wound larger than the face of a nickel.

When an ice storm or heavy snow breaks limbs in your trees you have a repair job to do. When an automobile or the power mower crashes into your tree, lacerating the bark and cutting into the wood, you have an emergency job on your hands. On examining your favorite birch tree you notice one limb with bracket fungi on it. Something has to be done. On occasion a lightning bolt strikes a tree, ripping away branches or bark or both. There is a chance that the tree might be saved. All of these occasions call for special techniques; in most cases you already have the proper tools to do the job.

Broken limbs and branches

When a branch breaks you are stuck with a hard decision—where to cut. Where NOT to cut is where ever a stub would be left. Where TO cut is at a crotch or at the point of origin of the damaged limb or branch. Which crotch? The one close to the break or further into the tree, depends on good drop pruning practice as suggested by the scaffold of branches. Refer to drop pruning diagram, page 36.

First, clear away the wreckage. If you have to get up into the tree, place your ladder firmly, sandbag the bottom rungs and tie the top rails to the tree. Put on non-skid gardening shoes and clothes that do not bind, and climb up to the damaged area. With a lopper, saw, or pole pruner (select the right tool for the diameter of the wood to be cut) cut away the branch **beyond** the break or split. Go no further until this piece is on the ground and out of the way. Now, you have a stubbed-back branch with a break in it. If it is of any size at all—say, over two inches in diameter, cut again just below the break. If it is a "tear down", that is, if a branch has pulled away from a crotch, ripping a piece of bark with it, carefully cut away the bark and get rid of the dangling stub.

Next, with good drop pruning in mind, look at the configuration of the tree. Should you go to the first crotch below the injury, make a drop pruning cut, and let it go at that or would the crown of the tree be in better balance if you were to come back another crotch or two into the tree before making your final cut. Usually it is best to save as much of the tree as possible.

There is another aspect. When one or more large limbs are lost due to catastrophe and they are taken down, the crown of the tree is badly out of balance. There are great holes, and the remaining limbs reach out gaunt and gawky.

In this case, schedule a thorough pruning job for early next summer—if it is summertime when the branches are lost, do a light drop pruning job immediately. The idea is to reproportion the entire tree. Drop prune to shorten the longest branches. Fairly extensive drop pruning may be carried out in early summer, but at any other time take it easy and come back for additional pruning early next summer. Heavy, out of season pruning almost always results in a great proliferation of waterspouts on trunk and main limbs, and then you have a real problem.

Bark injury

The hard, outer bark of a tree protects the soft, inner bark which carries food manufactured in the leaves down to feed the roots. Under the soft bark lies a paper-thin layer, the cambium, which is responsible for lateral growth, and the cambium covers the newest wood which carries water and minerals from the soil up to the branches and leaves. Small wonder that girdling a tree—that is, cutting a groove round the trunk—kills it quickly. Any injury that penetrates the hard outer bark is serious, the deeper it goes, and the more extensive it is, the greater the need for a quick repair job.

Exposed wood is especially susceptible to invasion by decay organisms and wood-boring insects. To correct trunk damage you must trim away all lacerated tissues, smooth exposed wood, providing quick drainage, and then seal the area.

Tree trunk repair work generally begins with a heavy pruning knife; the sort with a curved blade. If you do not have such a tool, substitute a linoleum knife, very similar in design, or use a stout-bladed, straight knife. Whatever your tool, it needs to be razor sharp. Trim away all torn and bruised bark. The ideal repair job ends up with a lozenge-shaped wound cut back to firm, uninjured bark, with the bark properly beveled toward the wood, and with the wound drawing to points top and bottom. Such a wound usually heals quickest.

With the bark repaired, turn your attention to the exposed wood. Use a draw knife or wood chisel to smooth the surface. If there are deep cuts, with a

5 general rules to follow when repairing a damaged tree

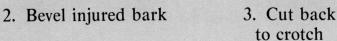

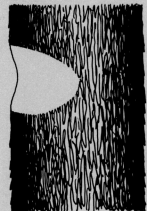

1. Knife trimming jagged stubs

2. Bevel injured bark

3. Cut back to crotch

gouge smooth these and cut away the lower lip so rainwater will drain away quickly. The finished job should be smooth and uninterrupted. Immediately spray the exposed surface and the bark margins with a very light application of tree wound dressing from an aerosol container or brush on a thin coating of dilute tree wound paint. After this first coating has hardened, apply another layer of dressing. From time to time, check the condition of the wound. If the paint is weathering, sand it smooth and apply more dressing. Cambium tissue at the margins of the wound will produce corky tissues that will bulge outward, eventually growing to cover the wound entirely.

Lightning injury

A lightning strike frequently is lethal. When lightning strikes directly into a tree, shattering the top and grounding through the trunk, the tree is almost sure to die within a short time even though considerable green top remains. Surprisingly enough, when lightning strikes a tree ripping a strip of bark from leafy crown to the soil line the tree can survive, probably because the intense electrical charge remained outside the body of the tree. But there is a nasty wound to repair. Proceed as best you can. Cut away shattered branches, keeping in mind the form of the tree. Always cut to a crotch or the trunk, never leave stubs. Dress all cuts as you proceed. Next, use chisels, gouges, and a drawknife to smooth ripped and splintered wood where ever possible. Sometimes this is a complicated job, but because the strike was from the top downward splinters stick upward and invite water and disease entry. Do the best job you can to smooth torn wood. Finally, trace out the margins of the wound to healthy bark. With a stout knife held in both hands, blade tipped slightly so the bark will be beveled, draw the knife in a neat straight or gently curving line separating injured bark from firm, healthy bark. Peel away the injured bark and do a final job of smoothing wood. Apply tree wound

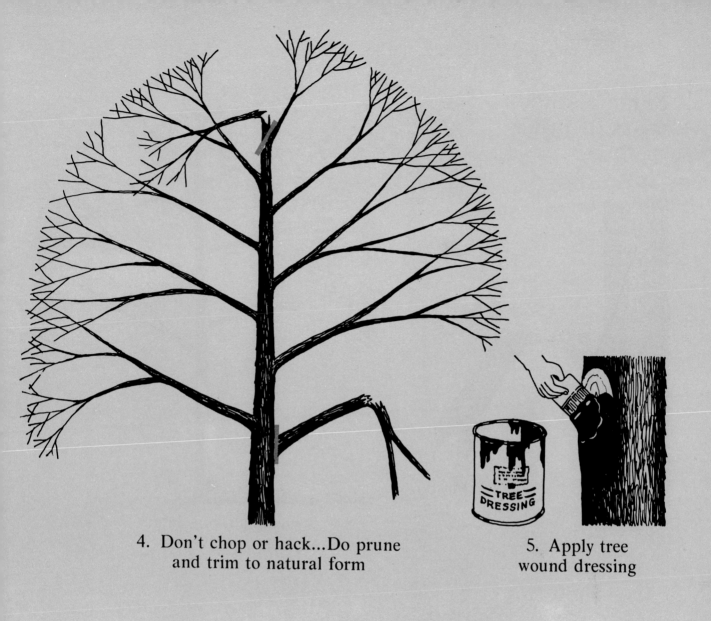

4. Don't chop or hack...Do prune
and trim to natural form

5. Apply tree
wound dressing

dressing, one or more layers, to insure a good seal.

Remember a lightning struck tree is in grave condition. It may live; it could die. With the wounds patched, apply fertilizer. A 1:2:1 ratio formulation is best. The readily available 5:10:5 garden fertilizer will do the job. The higher level of phosphate will stimulate new roots to replace those killed when the strike grounded, and the nitrogen is sufficient to encourage new leafy growth.

Fire injury

Occasionally a tree trunk is scorched by a building fire or a ground fire, or overhanging limbs are scorched by heat from an outdoor grill or trash burner. Heat injury is not always easy to spot unless obvious charring occurs. But bark can be killed as well as the cambium which underlies it. In the case of the tree trunk and large branches, this shows up as off-color bark, sunken or depressed bark (perhaps after a season or two), or even when bracket fungi begin to grow on the dead bark. If you know that a tree has been scorched, gingerly pare down to the soft bark and the cambium where you suspect injury and compare it with a similar "test hole" made on the healthy side of the tree. If you are convinced injury has occurred, proceed as with trunk abrasions. That is, pare away the bark, bevel it, preferably to a lozenge shape, and seal the exposed wood and bark margins. If charring has occurred you must cut deeply enough to reach healthy, uninjured tissues.

Usually the first sign of heat injury to overhead branches is withered leaves that cling to the branchlets. With a pole pruner nip off a small sample branch and examine the lower side of it. Sometimes only the leaves, themselves, have been damaged by the heat. But if the juicy, shiny bark of the twigs is, on the undersides, shrunken or shrivelled, lifeless-looking, the injury is more serious. The best solution for this condition is to drop prune, removing the scorched branches at appropriate crotches. Don't forget to seal the cuts.

Some common
types of injury

Broken limb

Lightning injury

Wire girdling, inclusions, and branch stubs

A tree trunk becomes larger in diameter by the annual addition of new wood and bark from the outside. If an object is fastened to a tree trunk—say, a fence is nailed to it—eventually the new layers of bark and wood will engulf it. It is not uncommon to see wire fencing which was stapled to a sapling protruding from the center of a now sizeable tree. Nails driven into a tree trunk, screw eyes for swings or clotheslines, tools hung on a branch, and even dead branches left as broken stubs, become engulfed into the trunk of the tree.

While a tree usually survives these foreign inclusions, they cannot be healthy for it. And when the tree has to come down foreign bodies are a real danger to the man using the power saw. With single strand wire, the best bet is to cut it off at both sides of the tree and hope that it will gradually be consumed as a source of iron by the trunk. Other objects should be dug out with as little injury to the

tree as possible. Always trim the bark carefully and smooth and shape the wood for good downward drainage, then seal all cut surfaces. For the sake of future generations, keep solid objects away from your trees so they do not become embedded in the wood.

One documented incident dealing with an embedded inclusion involves an iron cannon ball, presumably fired at hostile Indians on the Pacific Northwest coast by Captain Frobisher, Vancouver or some other explorer. The ball struck into a tree and became engulfed in the wood. When the giant tree was felled and the log went to the sawmill the giant circle saw blade exploded as it caught on the long buried ball, and fragments of the blade killed several mill workers busy nearby.

Girdling roots

Occasionally a new root develops late in the life of a tree just where the trunk enters the ground. Such a root may grow sideways and in doing so, wrap itself

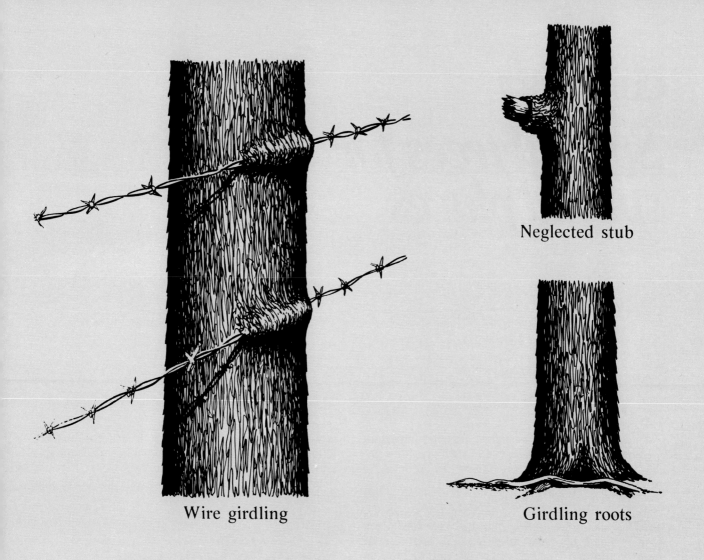

Neglected stub

Wire girdling

Girdling roots

around the tree trunk or around main supporting roots. As this strange root grows in diameter it may actually strangle the tree trunk or the larger roots it crosses. If you notice a root growing round the tree trunk just at the ground line, with a light shovel dig away the soil to expose its origin. Cut it away, seal the wound, and dig out the root. If your tree is growing weakly despite suitable growing conditions and ample fertilizer and water, peel back the sod from its base and do some exploratory digging with a trowel or small shovel. Chances are you will find a girdling root.

Dieback, disease and insect-ridden branches

Have you ever looked up into your favorite tree and noticed an obviously unhealthy limb or even a dead one, that apparently appeared overnight? The unhealthy condition may have developed over a considerable period, but we fail to notice what takes place overhead in the garden. Secure your ladder in the tree and climb up to investigate the problem. If the limb is obviously insect ridden throughout, or if all its leaves are flagged and drooping, your best choice is to do a drop pruning job, removing that entire limb immediately.

Once in a while an entire limb shows wilted or off-color foliage for no apparent reason. With the pole pruner take samples and do some investigation. Select a pencil-sized twig with badly wilted or discolored leaves and with a sharp knife skin back the bark. Is the wood beneath the same color as that of a healthy twig taken from a nearby branch? Are there off-color streaks that do not appear in healthy twigs? Cut across the branchlet and examine the cut surface. Is the wood uniformly off-white or are there dots of discolored tissue? Perhaps the larger parts of the branch may show small holes in the bark indicating an invasion of boring insects. Better take a generous bundle of **fresh** material to the County Extension office and ask the experts to analyze your problem. In any case, there is every reason to cut out obviously unhealthy branches, using appropriate drop pruning and cut repair techniques.

CHAPTER 7

Special trees for special places

Trees with weeping branches become important features in the garden. Because of their special form, they attract attention. They should be groomed to perfection.

When you prune a weeping tree, you have two objects to keep in mind. Thin your tree's weeping branches carefully so they are not crowded. Each branch should be a part of the overall architectural form of the tree. Second, allow the tree to grow in height gradually. Many gardeners panic when a branch in a weeping tree sticks up in the center of the tree, and they cut it off. But these upright branches (so long as they are part of the weeping crown and not breaks from the original stem stock) will eventually build your tree into a series of cascading tiers. Leave one or two of them.

These upright shoots, reaching above the drooping branches of the tree, will in turn produce another crop of weeping branches. Every summer prune through your weeping tree, removing all underneath branches that are being shaded out, and trim away all weak or dead branches.

Among the best weeping trees for home gardens are the weeping flowering cherries, the weeping flowering crabapples, the sterile form of weeping mulberry called 'Chaparral', and less common decumbent forms such as the weeping Japanese pagoda tree or the weeping 'Camperdown' elm. One of the most elegant of the weepers is the purple-leaved weeping beech, and the green leaved form is equally beautiful.

Weeping birches are a special case. These develop naturally with a minimum of pruning. They require little thinning or topwork. An occasional injured or weak branch has to be pruned from a birch tree, but you will notice that, even with careful cutting followed by proper attention to wound dressing, the scar heals badly. The rule with birches is to prune them as little as possible. They are far better left alone.

Specially built trees

Trees with ball-shaped heads are particularly useful in the restricted space of a small garden, but these very formal forms have to be used carefully as they do not fit into a casually designed garden. Some require very severe annual pruning; the umbrella catalpa, so much favored at the turn of the century, is one of these. Every spring cut last year's branches back to the shortest possible stubs. Buds will break from the old wood and each will make a several feet long leafy shoot. Thus, the top of the umbrella catalpa is totally renewed every spring. In some areas, the cutting back is done in the fall.

Globe locusts and other hard-twigged globe headed trees require far less pruning. Each summer clip new growth back to half its length or less, with an eye toward maintaining a uniform ball-shape. If branches seem to be crowded, with a lopper reach in and take out a branch here and there. If you restrict the new growth of your globe-shaped ornamental or flowering tree right from the beginning you will get many years of ornamental value from it. But if you allow it to make long, whippy shoots while young in order to get a quick display, the branches will be weak and the useful life of the plant will be reduced to a few years.

For the root system a healthy, reliable sort is the

Mazzard strain. To that almost any ornamental top could be grafted. For year round beauty try a long, unbranched whip of **Prunus serrula,** the Birch Bark cherry with brilliantly shining, papery bark. Grow this on to the desired height, then bud on a crown of 'Amanogawa' Japanese cherry to make an almost columnar top (bearing in mind the vehicular street traffic). The result is a three-part tree with strong, deep roots, a clean, high, beautifully ornamental trunk and a specially shaped, floriferous crown. The tree has been tailor-made to fit a special case.

Specially built trees are becoming more familiar every day at nurseries throughout the country.

New faces for oldies

Other alternatives are possible. Special selections of old familiar trees can be restricted in height so they fit beneath overhead wires. Specially grown specimens of familiar ornamentals give a new dimension to a favorite plant (for instance, Japanese tree lilac grown as a tall, single stem with a well formed head of branches and great panicles of white flowers at the top). Even the familiar Weeping mulberry, scorned by most gardeners because its fruits and seedlings cause a major maintenance problem, has a new face. It is almost a carbon copy as far as form goes but it is the male selection and though it flowers, it bears no fruit or seed.

You probably will not want to landscape your entire lot with these highly specialized selections. But for special problem areas, and to break up the monotony of a vast lawn where several trees are to grow, color variants and special growth forms broaden the spectrum of materials from which to choose.

What to do when your specialty shaped tree arrives

Special tree forms seldom come fully shaped as they are expensive to propagate and costly to grow on in the nursery. Don't be surprised if your fastigiate maple or columnar ash is just a stick when it arrives. Plant it carefully, stake it and do some judicious pruning as it develops, always building toward the special form it is supposed to take.

"Built-up" trees are even more lank and unhandsome when newly purchased. Usually they are shipped bare-root and with a good but minimal top. When the plants arrive soak them—roots, stem and top—overnight. Plant them in an oversized, deeply dug hole and fill around them with good loam enriched with damp brown peat or leafmold. Scratch a little superphosphate into the soil area below the roots. Use no nitrogenous fertilizers the first year and allow no manures or chemical fertilizers to touch the exposed roots. Support them with a heavy post or three guys. Use wires run through pieces of rubber hose at the tree. You may water these in with a high phosphate transplant fertilizer or with a Transplantone solution. Give them a thorough watering once each week through summer if the weather is dry.

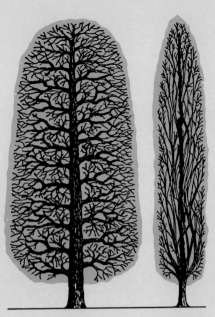

Columnar
Strong central
trunk with
uniform, stubby
branching

Fastigiate
Crown composed
of strongly
ascending
branches

Pyramidal-Conical
Cone-shaped silhouette

Weeping Forms
Main branches grow laterally
and become pendulous; young
twigs are completely decumbent

Partial listing of tree forms

Upright-growing (fastigiate) flowering and ornamental trees

Columnar Weeping Birch,
Betula pendula 'Fastigiata'

Columnar Ironwood,
Carpinus caroliniana 'Pyramidalis'

Pyramidal Hornbeam,
C. betulus 'Columnaris'

Columnar Hornbeam,
C. betulus 'Fastigiata'

Katsura,
Cercidiphyllum japonicum

Columnar Flowering Dogwood,
Cornus florida 'Fastigiata'

Columnar Single-seed Hawthorn,
Crataegus monogyna 'Stricta'

Columnar Washington Thorn,
C. phaenopyrum 'Fastigiata'

Columnar Golden Rain-tree,
Koelreuteria paniculata 'Fastigiata'

Columnar Siberian Crabapple,
Malus baccata 'Columnaris'

Columnar Pearleaf Crabapple,
M. prunifolia 'Fastigiata'

Columnar Cherry Crabapple,
M. x-robusta 'Erecta'

Van Eseltine Crabapple,
M. 'Van Eseltine'

Columnar Sargent Cherry,
Prunus sargentii 'Columnaris'

Amanogawa Cherry,
P. serrulata 'Amanogawa'

Columnar Mountain-ash,
Sorbus aucuparia 'Fastigiata'

Upright-growing (fastigiate) shade trees

Columnar Norway Maple,
Acer platanoides 'Columnare'

Upright Norway Maple,
A. platanoides 'Erectum'

Upright Sycamore-maple,
A. pseudoplatanus 'Erectum'

Columnar Red Maple,
A. rubrum 'Columnare'

Temple's Upright Sugar Maple,
A. saccharum 'Temple's Upright'

Newton Sentry Maple,
A. saccharum 'Newton Sentry'

Columnar European Beech,
Fagus sylvatica 'Fastigiata'

Columnar Maidenhair Tree,
Ginkgo biloba 'Fastigiata'

Columnar Tulip-tree, *Liriodendron
tulipiferum* 'Fastigiatum'

Pyramidal White Poplar,
Populus alba 'Pyramidalis'

Lombardy Poplar, *P. nigra* 'Italica'

Columnar Simon Poplar,
P. simonii 'Fastigiata'

Columnar Swedish Poplar,
P. tremula 'Erecta'

Columnar English Oak,
Quercus robur 'Fastigiata'

Columnar Black Locust,
Robinia pseudoacacia 'Erecta'

Bald-cypress, *Taxodium distichum*

Columnar Basswood,
Tilia americana 'Fastigiata'

Swedish Upright Linden,
T. cordata 'Swedish Upright'

Columnar Big-leaf Linden,
T. platyphyllos 'Fastigiata'

Columnar Silver Linden,
T. tomentosa 'Erecta'

Augustine Elm,
Ulmus americanus 'Augustine'

Roundheaded
Large, bell-shaped crown on straight trunk

Globeheaded
Small, tight ball-shaped crown on straight trunk.
For details on special construction of these
forms see page 52.

Dampier Elm,
U. carpinifolia 'Dampieri'

Weeping and pendulous trees

Weeping White Birch,
Betula pendula

Cutleaf Weeping Birch,
B. pendula 'Gracilis'

Purple-leaf Weeping Birch,
B. pendula 'Purple Splendor'

Young's Weeping Birch,
B. pendula 'Youngii'

Weeping White Dogwood,
Cornus florida 'Pendula'

Weeping Hawthorn,
Crataegus monogyna 'Pendula'

Weeping Birch,
Fagus sylvatica 'Pendula'

Weeping Purple Birch,
F. sylvatica 'Purpureo-pendula'

Weeping European Ash,
Fraxinus excelsior 'Pendula'

Weeping Golden-chain tree,
Laburnum anagyroides 'Pendula'

Echtermeyer (Pink Weeping)
Crab Apple, *Malus*
'Oekonomierat Echtermeyer'

Red Jade Crabapple,
M. 'Red Jade'

Chaparral Mulberry (non-fruiting),
Morus alba 'Chaparral'

Weeping Flowering Peach,
Prunus persica
'Weeping Double Red'

Weeping Sargent Cherry,
P. sargentii 'Pendula'

Weeping Japanese Cherry,
P. serrulata 'Ukon'

Weeping Higan Cherry,
P. subhirtella 'Pendula'

Golden Weeping Willow,
Salix alba 'Tristis'

Babylon Weeping Willow,
S. babylonica

Niobe Weeping Willow,
S. x *blanda*

Thurlow Weeping Willow,
S. x *elegantissima*

Weeping Japanese Pagoda Tree,
Sophora japonica 'Pendula'

Weeping Mountain-ash,
Sorbus aucuparia 'Pendula'

Weeping Basswood,
Tilia americana 'Pendula'

Camperdown Elm,
Ulmus glabra 'Camperdownii'

Weeping Scotch Elm,
U. glabra 'Pendula'

Globeheaded forms

Almira Norway Maple,
Acer pliatanoides 'Almira'

Globeheaded Norway,
Acer platanoides 'Globosum'

Tilford Red Maple,
Acer rubrum 'Tilford'

Globe Hawthorn,
Crataegus monogyna 'Compacta'

Globeheaded Blue Ash,
Praxinus excelsior 'Globosa'

Scanlon Globe Cherry,
Prunus avium 'Scanlon'

Flowering Globe Locust,
Robinia hispida 'Macrophylla'

Globe Locust,
Robinia pseudoacacia 'Umbraculifera'

How a specialty tree is 'built'...
from the ground up

The nurseryman "builds" a weeping tree in most instances. For example, the typical weeping Japanese cherry tree is put together as follows. A batch of mahaleb or other very hardy, vigorously rooting cherry tree seedlings are grown.

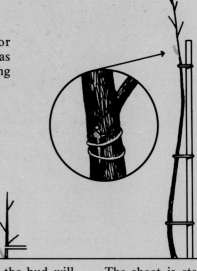

The seedlings may be lifted for grading, or they may be used in the row where the seed was sown after they have grown for a year.

After midsummer, a bud of a strong upright strain of cherry is inserted in the bark of the seedling close to the ground. This bud "takes", that is, its cells fuse with the cells of the seedling.

Next spring the bud will open to make a strong shoot and the top of the seedling will be cut off. That leaves the seedling root system with a different leafy shoot growing on it.

The shoot is staked upright and when it reaches a height of six feet or more another bud is grafted into its bark high up. This bud comes from weeping cherry stock.

Pruning special trees in special situations

Weeping trees

Many unusual forms of shade and ornamental trees can meet special needs on your grounds and unlike topiary, hedges and arbors they require no special pruning to achieve the desired form.

Today many unusual forms of shade and ornamental trees to fit any space requirement are available . Take the Lombardy poplar. It is just a fastigiate (upright) form of the Italian counterpart of the wide-spreading native Cottonwood. The weeping mulberry tree is an oldtime selection of the common variety. For a variety of color variations, take the beech trees. They can be considered where a large spread of lawn needs to be relieved from the monotony of green. There are copper and purple leaved forms; an aurea form with yellowish-green foliage; a tricolor form of variegated purple, pink, white and greenish-purple. And too, there's a choice of leaf forms. There is the regular, long, narrow or ribbon-like shape available. The beeches also come in a variety of shapes: fastigiate (poplar-shaped), columnar (narrow upright), pyramidal (cone-shaped), standard, globe and weeping.

While not all trees come in such a variety of colors and shapes, color and form variants are known for most ornamental species and they provide a great deal of elasticity to your landscape.

There are particular situations, other than purely visual, which could require you to consider special trees or special shapes to solve a design problem. Take driveways, for example. A broad-spreading tree could interfere with driveway use and parking. You could turn to a narrow, upright form of the same tree and overcome the objection to its spreading characteristic which may be its only fault as far as you are concerned. Here are just a few suggestions.

You could turn to a narrow, upright form such as the fastigiate European hornbeam, a columnar Norway maple or an upright beech. For a flowering tree, there is the columnar form of the Siberian crabapple. If the stern, vertical lines of a columnar or fastigiate

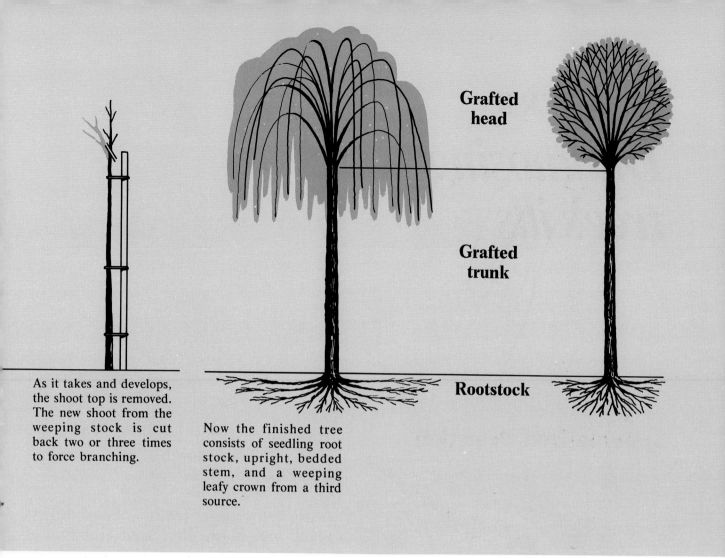

As it takes and develops, the shoot top is removed. The new shoot from the weeping stock is cut back two or three times to force branching.

Now the finished tree consists of seedling root stock, upright, bedded stem, and a weeping leafy crown from a third source.

Grafted head

Grafted trunk

Rootstock

specimen seem undesirable, you could select the restricted globe head of a globe locust, the globe hawthorn or one of the globe ash varieties. The foregoing are but a few examples. For further suggestions see the accompanying illustrations and tables.

Globe-shaped trees

Another way of solving a particular design problem is to use specially built trees. The technique of building trees to meet specific requirements has been known in the U.S. for some time. The fundamentals have been borrowed from European tree specialists and adapted to our needs.

As an example, take the parking between a street and a sidewalk where a nicely flowering ornamental tree is desired. The need is for a deep, vigorous root system that will not interfere with the pavements but will survive the cramped quarters. The tree should have a tall, clean stem that will hold branches not only clear of sidewalk passersby but clear of street traffic as well. A flowering Japanese cherry tree would be ideal for the show of spring bloom but these are relatively branched in most cases, their trunks are not particularly elegant and they may have weak root systems.

Columnar trees

Trees with sharply ascending branches such as the Lombardy poplar need little pruning in most cases. The poplars are a special case as they are very fast growing and with weak wood. When you plant a new poplar tree, cut it back almost to the ground. A little top growth will be made while the roots take hold; then the tree will regain all it lost in a season or two. While unpruned, newly planted poplars often survive, they are weak and unthrifty for years to follow. Early each spring prune back last year's shoots to one or two buds. Such heavy pruning produces a densely compact, very narrow tree of great ornamental value. As poplars tend to develop various twig cankers and blights, watch for lesions on the wood and prune out infected areas annually.

Other upright-growing trees such as the fastigiate English oak, the upright maples, hornbeams, the beeches and the 'Amanogawa' Japanese flowering cherry need far less pruning. While these are young, prune away any branch that tends to spread laterally, cutting to an *inside* bud. A bud on the inner side of the twig will produce an inward-growing shoot, and this in turn makes a tight, narrow tree. Never 'top' or head back a columnar tree as it will develop a broomy top.

CHAPTER 8
Diagnosing your tree's ills

Systematized detection

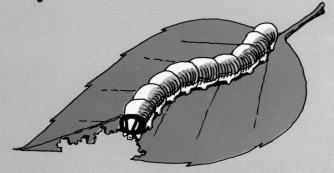

Is it an insect problem?

Look for gnawed leaves (evidence of chewing insect damage).

Look for small piercing-sucking insects on buds, backs of leaves, shoot tips. Malformed young leaves often indicate the presence of these.

Look for tiny gnawed fissures in crotches of twigs.

Look for small holes bored into twigs—split some twigs and look for larvae (grubs) under the bark or in the wood.

Examine the trunk for signs of borers, small exit holes, sawdust and, in some cases, loose bark.

With fruit-type trees (ornamental peach and plum, flowering crabapple) look for insects below the ground at the base of the trunk and on major roots.

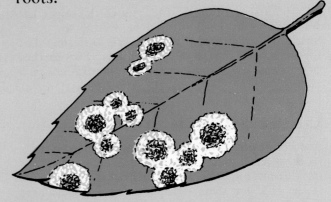

Is it a disease?

Examine leaves and shoots. Are there leaf spots, either sunken or raised? Is the tissue discolored? If spots are present, are there tiny specks in the middle indicating presence of fungus fruiting bodies (almost microscopic)?

Examine twigs and branches for signs of cankers (sunken patches with discolored bark). Is the bark dead? Are there pustules on the discolored bark or on the wood beneath it?

Examine the trunk for cankers, for bracket fungi or for running wounds.

Is it a physiological problem?

How good is the drainage?

If the leaves or twigs are twisted, stunted, abnormal, who has been using a broadleaf weed killer on a windy day?

If the summer foliage is yellow (a chlorotic condition), add iron (see under fertilizing) and observe results.

Is the color of the leaves wrong: irregular green—yellow patterns, reddish mottling, browning?

Did last winter's ice melting chemical (including the "harmless" sorts) drain into the tree's root zone?

Is there a gas line near the root zone of the tree? Has the grade been altered near the tree?

Your power of observation, combined with your knowledge of what the healthy tree should look like, will help you eliminate many possibilities of agents causing tree abnormalities. If you become completely stumped, phone the County Extension Agent and discuss the problem with him— but do not phone until you have made notes on all the above points because he will demand specific information.

Three types of sprayers for applying insecticides and fungicides

Trombone sprayer

Your tree is unthrifty; or perhaps it obviously is in trouble, with wilted, yellowed, or falling leaves, dieing branches, or peeling bark. What should you do? There is no simple answer. A case history of the tree is immensely helpful—if you can look over events in the tree's life for the past five or ten years you may discover something that may explain today's problems.

This is simplest with old, established trees. When a tree that has been going along in good shape year after year begins to look puny, usually it is not too difficult to isolate the cause. The problem may have to do with a biological invasion of some sort. That is, the tree may have a bacterial or fungal disease, it may be unwilling host to an insect infestation, or it **may have a virus. If the causal agent is not biological,** then it must be something in the environment.

Most commonly, environmental ills are underground but air pollutants are increasingly serious. Perhaps your tree has been subjected to a change of grade. Most established trees will not tolerate any significant change of grade within their root zone. Tree roots stratify themselves deeply enough to insure an almost constant moisture supply, but close enough to the surface to benefit from plentiful soil aeration. Add a layer of soil and this aeration is reduced, particularly with modern soil moving methods which result in extreme compaction due to the heavy machinery involved. Or, if soil has been peeled away, roots are over-aerated and in a zone that is subjected

to drought, heat and frost. A great many fine old trees are lost each year because today's people—especially construction people—do not understand the peril of altering the grade under a tree.

Another underground peril is toxic foreign chemicals. One of the commonest poisonous chemicals that kills tree roots is natural gas. Did you know that, in most soils, a buried gas pipe is not firmly embedded in soil? Rather, due to soil shrinkage and expansion, pipe vibration, and for other reasons, the pipe has a more or less continuous cylinder of space along its length. If a gas leak occurs anywhere in the pipe, this air space fills with gas. Quite commonly leaks occur at junctions from gas main to house feeder line, in the feeder line where it enters the foundation of the house, or at a meter. Eventually, natural gas saturates the soil, and trees (also shrubs and grass) die of asphyxiation. In most towns gas companies are very reluctant to admit that their product is loose in your soil, but they can be pushed into making tests with a soil probe instrument which immediately reveals the presence of gas in the soil.

Chemicals used in household chores, and particularly those used to keep sewer pipes free from obstructions, may be extremely toxic to trees. Sewer lines often are fractured for one reason or another (earth shift or settling, passage of a very heavy vehicle or machine, and so on) so that leaks occur. Roots grow toward leaking sewer lines, attracted by a constant moisture supply. Add poison to the liquid in the pipe and your tree is in trouble. It pays to know

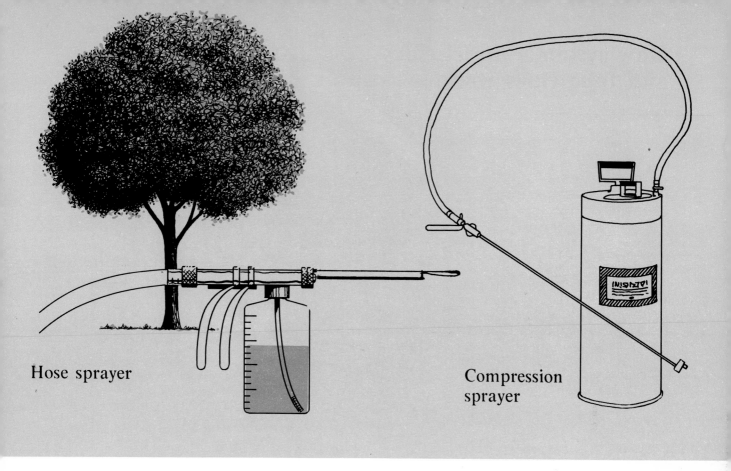

Hose sprayer

Compression sprayer

exactly where all buried utility lines cross the property.

Sometimes chemicals get into the soil from the surface—and you may be the guilty party who poisoned the tree. Ice melting compounds, salt, calcium chloride, and other agents, many of which are labeled "Safe for plants", often kill plants. These compounds, applied in winter to sidewalks and driveways, may drain off and puddle on top of partially frozen soil or seep into the soil to be held by an impervious layer just at the tree root zone. No problem occurs, usually, in winter or through the spring months when soil moisture is plentiful. But when dry summer weather comes along and the tree's water needs increase, sufficient quantities of the chemical may be taken in to cause leaf scorch, twig die-back, or even to kill a woody plant. The cure here is to use ice melting compounds only on surfaces constructed to drain into traps and sewers. Cut down on the amount of chemical by mixing with sand, part for part or even at a greater dilution. Do not substitute fertilizer as an ice melter. It does work efficiently, but, being soluble and being a salt compound, it, too, is extremely destructive as a concentrated solution. If your soil is extremely porous, and if your spring rains are copious, probably you do not have to worry about ice melting chemical damage to your plants because these soluble chemicals will be quickly washed down (leached) beyond the reach of tree roots. But on average soil, and particularly on tightly compacted, recently graded (within the past

five years) soil, such chemical injury is a real hazard.

Tree root injury caused by weed control chemicals is a common occurrence in modern gardens. The nonselective weed killers, arsenicals, creosotes, phenols, and the like, used to keep walks and drives free of weeds are sure to destroy all tree roots which lie beneath the area to which the chemical is applied. If the chemical happens to be one that is translocated from the root to any other part of the tree, considerable damage or total destruction may be anticipated.

The selective weed killers also injure tree roots. Anything that will kill a dandelion or chickweed will also kill a tree. More of the chemical is needed to kill the tree, but you may easily apply a lethal dosage by the time you have sprayed or applied granular material over the entire root zone of the tree. Sometimes these selective weed control chemicals work in a more subtle fashion. Each ensuing year more damage is done to the tree roots; tree growth slows and the foliage crop is thin, but the tree lives on. Finally the critical threshold is reached, or a very hot, dry summer comes along, and the tree dies. Or if it does not die, the tree top is filled with dead twigs and branches. General die-back through the top of a tree almost always is indicative of something wrong at the roots of the tree.

What can you do if you suspect trouble at the roots of your tree? First, try to reason out the problem. Is a gas or sewer line nearby? Has there been a change in grade? Has any chemical been applied nearby that may be in the soil around the tree roots? Was last

How systemic insecticides and fungicides work

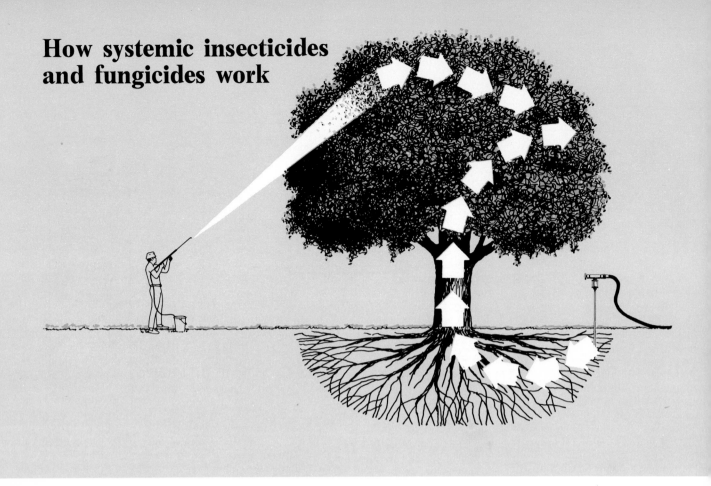

year a soggy one, and is there a chance that your tree stood in undrained soil and drowned? The next step calls for rolling back the sod in several places under the dripline of the tree for some spadework. Use a fork to loosen the soil and with a trowel carefully dig down to find some of the youngest, thread to string-sized tree roots. Are they crisp and brittle, white inside with a rubbery sort of outer covering (all of which indicates a healthy condition) or are they limp and lifeless, cores yellow to black, and with the outer cover sloughing off easily. If your tree roots are dead, the problem begins at that point, and you may have to call in an expert unless you are sure of damage due to any of the causes listed above.

If the tree still shows signs of life, try to save it. Turn the tree root feeder on full blast and plunge the shaft full depth into the soil, working it up and down rapidly. This makes deep, open holes for fast aeration (and drainage to at least the depth of the holes). Next, use the same tool and gently apply a high phosphate or tree transplant fertilizer throughout the root zone to encourage the rapid development of new roots. Finally, drop prune the top of the tree, taking out as much as a third or more of the leafy crown to balance the above-ground scaffold of branches to the reduced root system.

Not every dead or dying tree root system has been killed by compacted soil, soggy conditions, or a toxic chemical. Insect parasites and fungus diseases are all too common, and one of these may have attacked your tree. We never think of aphids on the roots of plants, but the wooly apple aphid, a vicious underground pest, has killed more than one flowering crabapple tree. Verticillium wilt attacks a wide range of ornamental and shade trees. The branch by branch die-back characteristic of this fungus disease could easily be mistaken for various non-biologically induced root problems. Refer to a plant pest and disease reference book such as Dr. Malcom Shurtleff's *How to Control Diseases and Pests of Trees and Shrubs*.

Your tree is far too valuable to lose while you play detective. It is commendable to try to figure out what is ailing your plant and in doing so to become a more informed gardener. It is practical to phone up the County Extension Agent or another professional tree expert and let an expert save your tree while you are sharpening up your knowledge of tree ailments.

Not every tree ill occurs below ground. Leaf spots and blights, twig diseases, branch cankers, and insect pests galore attack our garden trees. Your reference book will list common pests and diseases that attack many ornamentals, and suggest control practices within the scope of a home gardener. Your County Agent probably has lists of pests and diseases that are prevalent in your neighborhood and these, too, list control measures.

This matter of home pest and disease control is a touchy one. Good control chemicals exist that bring down almost any parasite, whether insect, fungus, or bacterium. The problem is matching the attacking organism with the proper control chemical—a control chemical that is reasonably safe for you to use. Before applying any chemical inform yourself fully as to what you are doing and what safety precautions are essential. Modern control chemicals are POISON-OUS. You don't have to swallow the stuff to take in a fatal dose. The fumes may get you. Some of these things absorb through your skin—they go through the cloth you are wearing, through your hide, into your bloodstream, and you have had it. Your reference library on disease and insect control chemicals cannot be too large, and you cannot spend too much time studying the information it contains. Pesticides and fungicides are valuable garden tools; use them correctly.

Certain tools help you apply parasite control chemicals to your trees. It is virtually beyond the capability of home spraying equipment to reach the top of a large shade tree. That is the job for a commercial tree spraying man. But there is good equipment that sprays to about twenty-five feet. Power sprayers, gasoline engine or electrically powered units, pump from a ten to twenty-five gallon tank to spray as much as eight to ten yards up. The long time favored trombone sprayer, a hand and arm powered affair which siphons your spray chemical preparation from a pail, is a very handy gadget. For knocking webworms, tent caterpillars, walnut datanas, and other clumped-up pests from high in a tree the trombone sprayer is hard to beat.

Your hose attached tree root feeder is another handy tool. You can buy cartridges which contain systemic insecticides, and soon at least one fungicide may be in cartridge form. For small trees these parasite controlling chemicals are hard to beat. A systemic chemical is one that you put in the soil (sometimes on the leaves) which is then taken into the plant and carried throughout its parts. A systemic insecticide then will kill any insect that bites into the tree. A systemic fungicide will kill susceptible fungi that occur within the plant tissues. Being underground, the chemical is of little danger to you, the gardener, to your pets, or to visiting birds or squirrels. By all means, look over the stock of systemic pesticide cartridges at your garden shop to see if the packages list controls for problems that occur in your garden.

Always remember that pesticides and fungicides are poisonous. Handle them very carefully. Spray so chemical drift does not get on your skin or on your clothing. When the application job is finished, take care to clean your equipment thoroughly. Begin with a water flush, and dispose of the waste material in a gravelled walk, an earthern sump, or in a well-flushed sewer. Rinse the equipment with a strong vinegar solution, then with a strong ammonia solution. The acid and the alkali will dissolve or perhaps deactivate residues of the pesticides. Flush with clear water, set the equipment in an airy place to dry, and, finally, before storing apply grease or oil to all moving parts and gasket dressing or neatsfoot oil to pump leathers. Taking care of the equipment used to take care of your tree is, in the long run, taking care of the tree.

CHAPTER 9
When to call for help

Inevitably the time comes when you have to summon outside tree care help. Try to work in such a way that it is not when your ladder has fallen and you are dangling by one foot caught in the crotch of a tree. There are some jobs related to tree care that are beyond the capabilities of the home gardener. Professional men have to be called in. Here are a few cases where it pays to call for help.

Approximate amount of spray material required for trees of different sizes		
Height in Feet	Spread in Feet	Gallons Per Application
4	3	up to ½
5	6	3
6	8	4
7	10	5
8	12	6
9	14	7
10	16	8
11	18	10
13	20	12
16	24	13
19	26	14
25	30	15
30	35	20
35*	38	25

*Trees above the height of 30-35 feet are best sprayed by a commercial arborist with a high-pressure sprayer. Trees sprayed early in the season require only about ⅓ of the spray needed in full leaf.

Spraying large trees

Spray equipment with sufficient power to do a thorough job of coating upper and lower surfaces of leaves high in the crown of a tall tree is heavy duty. Pumps work at two to four hundred pounds pressure and throw several gallons of spray solution or emulsion per minute. Some companies now use giant directional fans called mist blowers to impel/minute droplets of relatively concentrated solution or emulsion into the leaf zone. Large, commercial spray rigs can spray your trees effectively. You cannot begin to do a satisfactory job. When spraying is essential, call for help.

Cabling and bracing branches

This is a job that many home gardeners tackle, and often they get away with it. Not because they know what they are doing, but because trees are remarkably flexible and tolerant of abuse. To reinforce a weak or split crotch, to pull a torn limb back into place and secure it, is work for a trained technician. Often it means climbing high into a tree. And, high tree climbing is no task for an amateur. It means boring through the limb to be supported and the limb or limbs which are to support it, and this has to be done with a minimum of damage to the tree. It means having on hand plates, threaded tree bolt metal in various diameters and lengths, with or without eyes on the ends. It means having wire rope, and it means knowing how to use it properly. An amateur, with the best of intentions, will climb into a storm weakened tree top, screw a threaded hook or eye into a limb, loop a piece of wire around it, and pull it through another eye on a nearby limb. He is lucky if he gets out of the tree before wind rocks the branches, whipping the shallowly threaded eye bolt through the tree top with the force of a slingshot. Cabling and bracing is work for experts who know what materials to use, how to use them, and how to work safely.

Wetwood bleeding

Some trees,—notably elms but also others—, often drip noisome, foaming exudate from a crotch or a wound. This oozing is due to a condition called "wet wood". A biological ferment is occurring in the heartwood of the tree, activated by invading microörganisms. The solution to the problem lies in inserting pipe drains into the infected area to drain off the fermenting liquid and to permit air to enter. It takes considerable experience to know the approximate dimensions of the infected area, to know where to drill in order to insert the drain, and to know how to drill against pressure with some degree of safety. Of course, such drains must be properly positioned, inner end just into the infected area, pipe slanting slightly downward, and so on. This, again, is work for a qualified tree technician.

Cavity repair

Here is a debatable one. Some tree maintenance companies make a real operation out of mending a cavity in a tree. And yet, the woods are full of hollow trees that are growing quite nicely. It is worth noting that forest trees, as individuals, never feel the full

Spraying tall trees

Cabling and bracing

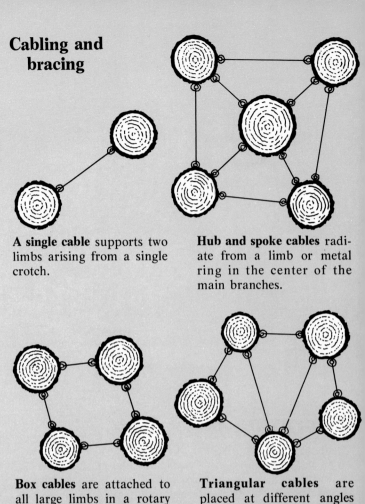

A single cable supports two limbs arising from a single crotch.

Hub and spoke cables radiate from a limb or metal ring in the center of the main branches.

Box cables are attached to all large limbs in a rotary manner.

Triangular cables are placed at different angles to each other.

blast of the wind. A free-standing hollow tree might conceivably be broken over or blown down in a high wind. Botanists sometimes challenge the wisdom of filling a tree with tons of concrete. They say that such a cold, moisture-holding mass eventually speeds up internal decay. If your tree has a hollow limb or trunk, you might take a middle course. Have someone do a very good job with chisels and gouges of removing all decay, right down to healthy wood. If the cavity is external, carve it for direct outward and downward drainage. Then seal the exposed, healthy wood with a fungus inhibitor-containing tree wound dressing. Leave the cavities clean but unfilled. Who is to do this work? If you have the time and patience, as well as a good tool kit, obviously you can do it yourself. So long as it is a job you can reach from the ground there is no great danger.

But if the cavity is high in the tree, or if you feel your expertise is not up to the demands of the operation, call in a specialist in tree cavity work. To locate a specialist you can check with your city forester or arborist; another source might be your county extension agent; in many communities the telephone Yellow Pages list under "Tree Service" a grouping of tree firms belonging to one or two national professional organizations (the International Shade Tree Conference and/or the National Arborist Association).

Restricted control chemicals

Several insecticides and a fungicide or two presently are marketed for application by trained technicians only. Theoretically, only trained technicians can get hold of these materials. But in every neighborhood there is a man who knows a man who can get restricted use chemicals. You can get these preparations if you try. It is about like getting a hand grenade. Certain chemicals are restricted because of their extremely hazardous nature. Leave them alone. If you want them applied to your tree (almost always they are trunk injected with a sort of self-operating syringe) call a man who is licensed in their use. Have him install them and have him come back and collect the capsules for disposal.

Commercial pruning specifications

When you hire a professional tree maintenance man to work on your high shade trees you should have a very clear understanding with him about the job. If he operates according to the standards set by the National Arborist Association he may hand you a

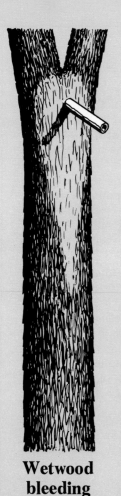

Wetwood bleeding

Cavity repair

card that spells out the work he intends to do. Lack of agreement between homeowner and arborist often results in incorrectly pruned trees or in mutual dissatisfaction with the financial arrangements. As the homeowner you need to find out from the professional what he intends to do and how much you are to pay for the specified work.

Arborists have set up categories of pruning; these enable you to understand what sort of pruning the man will do on your tree.

Fine pruning

Fine pruning includes the removal of dead, dieing, diseased, interfering, objectionable, and weak branches. These branches will be removed from the main trunks and limbs inside the leaf area and also any that extend beyond that area. The pruning will be completed according to the following specifications:

a. All cuts will be made close to the parent stem so healing will proceed rapidly under normal conditions.

b. All limbs one inch across or larger will be precut to prevent splitting. All branches 3½ inches in diameter or larger will be lowered to the ground with ropes.

c. All crossed or rubbing limbs will be removed where practical (where the removal will not leave large holes in the contour outline of the tree).

d. All old and new cuts over one inch in diameter will be painted with an approved tree wound dressing.

e. Where trees are known to be diseased, tools will be disinfected with alcohol after each cut but only if there is a chance that a disease will be transmitted by contaminated tools.

f. Old cuts and scars that have not healed properly and where callus growth is not already established will be traced and painted.

g. All girdling roots that show above the ground will be handled as follows:

● The root will be severed at both ends, or

● The root will be notched in the center with a chisel, or

● The root will be removed entirely without injury to bark or other part of the tree, or

● The presence of girdling roots will be reported to the owner.

h. All structural weaknesses, decayed trunk or branches, split crotches or branches will be reported to the owner.

Medium pruning

Medium pruning consists of coping with all branch problems covered in the first paragraph above, and the work will be done as specified in items a, b, d, e, f, g, and h. That is, medium pruning does not include removal of crossing and rubbing branches, but accounts for all other work to be done in fine pruning.

Safety pruning

Safety pruning removes only dead, diseased or weak branches that, if they were to fall, would be large enough to injure a person. The work is to be done according to fine pruning specifications a, b, d, e, and h. An additional specification is added, a suggested minimum for safety pruning. Remove dead or weak limbs over 2½ inches in diameter and 5 feet in length. Take into account the location of the tree (for example, a weak limb over a sitting terrace or sidewalk is more hazardous than one over a lawn or flower bed) and the species.

Cut-back pruning

Cut-back pruning is sometimes called "topping" but not at all synonomous with the always to be avoided stubbing back of major branches.

Cut-back pruning reduces the leafy top of a tree, and/or the sides, and under branches or individual limbs may be included. In reducing the overall size of a tree, shortening branches, and reducing leafy growth, the following items should be considered:

When cutting back branches, drop prune to a crotch and avoid cutting back to small suckers. Remove smaller limbs and twigs so that remaining foliage is evenly distributed.

Reduce the volume (size) of the tree overall to maintain a typical and symmetrical appearance.

On thin barked trees remove sufficient limbs and leafy growth to account for a good pruning job but avoid admitting too much sunlight below the crown (as limbs and trunk may be scalded). Some thin barked trees are lindens, sugar maples, red maples, beeches, apple trees, and oaks. One way to avoid potential injury is to complete the pruning during a dormant season.

When reducing the size of a tree, keep it shapely, and maintain a conformation typical of the species or cultivar.

When removing lower (under) limbs for clearance, take care to keep the tree symmetrical and do not remove limbs so large that normal sap flow will be inhibited.

In general, the total size of a tree should not be reduced by more than one-third in a single season.

When reducing the size of a tree, work according to the standards suggested under Fine Pruning practices.

Terms that apply to pruning

Callus—New tissue originating from the cambium layer (just under the bark) that will cover over a wound or a cut.

Cambium—A cylinder of tissue separating the bark and wood that is responsible for the annual increase in girth of a tree. It produces new wood cells and new bark cells.

Cut—Exposed wood that shows after a branch has been removed.

Cut-back—Reduction in the total top growth of a tree.

Dormant—A state of no active growth, as during the winter months.

Drop-pruning—The removal of a branch at a crotch. When a tree is to be thinned (cut back) drop-pruning is the only acceptable method of taking branches from the leafy crown.

Girdling Roots—Roots growing closely round the trunk of a tree just above or below the ground. These roots eventually will strangle the tree.

Healing—Occurs when callus tissue covers a cut.

Precut—The removal of a branch at least six inches from the parent stem as a safety precaution to avoid bark tear-down. Following the precut the stub is removed.

Scar—Natural or man-made lesions penetrating the bark of a tree so the wood is exposed.

Sucker—Vigorously growing abnormally placed shoots that break from main branches, trunk or even from roots.

Tear-down—Occurs when a large branch is cut close to the parent trunk or limb; as the cut weakens the wood, the branch sags, ripping away bark and wood to create a nasty wound that is difficult to repair and slow to heal. A precut will prevent a tear-down.

Thinning—The removal of live branches by drop-pruning to create more space in the crown of a tree.

Topping—Stubbing back main limbs. This is a horticulturally unacceptable technique because it creates ugly trees and invites insect infestations and disease.

Tracing—Cutting away the bark from the edges of a wound following the sap flow pattern. This encourages rapid callus production and results in early healing of a wound.

CHAPTER 10
Tree selection guide

Ornamental and Shade Trees of Small Stature
appropriate for city gardens and residential streets

Common Name	Botanical Name	Ultimate Height Hardy	Comment
Trident Maple	*Acer buergerianum*	35 feet to -5° F.	A small-leaved, craggy oriental maple of considerable charm. Good fall color.
Hornbeam Maple	A. carpinifolium	30 feet to -5° F.	With unlobed leaves (resembling those of hornbeam), this Japanese maple produces several upright trunks making a vase-shaped specimen. No fall color.
Vine Maple	A. circinatum	25 feet to -5°F.	A twisty, craggy Pacific Northwest native resembling the Japanese maple. Grows well in partial shade. Brilliant fall color.
Amur Maple	A. ginnala	20 feet to -50° F.	An open-headed, graceful North China species with beautiful, small leaves that color brightly in autumn. Fine specimen.
Rocky Mountain Maple	A. glabrum	25 feet to 0° F.	Small, rather upright-growing tree with sugar maple-like leaves 3 to 5 inches across that turn bright yellow in fall. Best grown in the western states.
Paperbark Maple	A. griseum	25 feet to -10° F.	Notable only for its beautifully bright cinnamon-colored bark that peels away in handsome patterns. The trifoliate leaves are nondescript. No fall color.
Fullmoon Maple	A. japonicum	25 feet to -10° F.	A beautiful Japanese species with a mounded crown, often irregular, of crowded leaves with 7 to 11 lobes. There are fine cultivars of this species. Brilliant fall color.
Manchurian Maple	A. mandshuricum	30 feet to -20° F.	An Asiatic species with spreading branches and an open crown. Leaves are trifoliate, red petioles in summer. Bright red fall color

Common Name	Botanical Name	Ultimate Height Hardy	Comment
Nikko Maple	*A. nikoense*	25 feet to -5° F.	With pinnately compound leaves, this Japanese species is vase-shaped. Beautiful red-to-plum fall color.
Japanese Maple	*A. palmatum*	20 feet to -10° F.	An Oriental species with 5 to 11 lobed leaves often tinted, colored, or of irregular form. One of the most ornamental of all garden trees for specimen use. Many cultivars of exotic character are available.
Globe Norway Maple	*A. platanoides* 'Globosum'	6 to 8 feet to -25° F.	For special, very formal planting, the dense ball-shaped head is grafted on a 6 to 8 foot trunk. Must be kept tightly pruned. Not for the usual, informal garden. No fall color.
Globe Sugar Maple	*A. saccharum* 'Globosum'	6 to 8 feet to -25° F.	Much like the Globe Norway Maple, but may be allowed to grow more loosely and irregularly (with careful annual pruning). A special tree best reserved for formal planting. May have fall color resembling the sugar maple.
Tatarian Maple	*A. tataricum*	30 feet to -15° F.	A small European-Asiatic species with an upright egg-shaped head of dense, small-lobed leaves. Rather a formal tree, fine for neighborhood street plantings. Good fall color, red and yellow.
Tschonoski Maple	*A. tschonoskii*	20 feet to -10° F.	A Japanese species of graceful form; twiggy, with small, 5-lobed leaves that turn bright yellow in the fall.
Hong Kong Orchid Tree	*Bauhinia blakeana*	20 feet to 40° F.	An evergreen, leguminous tree with spreading crown and bluish-green leaves like an ox foot. Flowers to 6 inches across, rose-purple or crimson, fragrant through winter months. Prune to thin occasionally.
Butterfly Bauhinia	*B. monandra*	25 feet to 40° F.	Rather similar to the above in form, but flowers more fragile, pale pink, appearing in spring. The foliage falls over winter.
Purple Bauhinia	*B. purpurea*	30 feet to 40° F.	An Indian species, should be lightly pruned heading back vigorous new growth every year or two. Flowers small, 3 to 5 inches across, white to purple, fragrant.
Orchid-tree	*B. variegata*	20 feet to 40° F.	A beautiful south Asian tree with lavender to purple flowers in loose clusters. Foliage falls irregularly. Like all Bauhinias, large seed pods may be messy. There is a pure white form of this.

Common Name	Botanical Name	Ultimate Height Hardy	Comment
Gray Birch	*Betula populifolia*	30 feet to -15° F.	The only birch that does not grow too large for this category (though European and Canoe Birches often are misplanted as small trees), this tree tolerates poor soil. It has white bark with black markings. Short-lived, like other birches should be pruned as little as possible.
American Hornbeam	*Carpinus caroliniana*	35 feet to -40° F.	A fine native species with smooth, gray bark that has a muscular look. With foliage like small elm leaves, this makes up into an open-headed, very attractive tree. Fall color is dark purplish red.
Oriental Hornbeam	*C. orientalis*	25 feet to -10° F.	A slow-growing species with small, narrowly ovate leaves, serrate, coloring red in the autumn. From a stubby trunk several strong branches grow laterally, then turn upright forming a most curious specimen.
Redbud	*Cercis canadensis*	35 feet to -30° F.	Handsome native species, best grown as an irregularly shaped specimen or planted in a small grove. Tolerates shade. Prune over older trees removing weak branches and thin crowded areas in the crown. Clear pink and pure white forms are available.
California Redbud	*C. occidentalis*	15 feet to 10° F.	Similar to the above but smaller, less hardy, and leaves notched at the tips. Deserves wider use.
Raceme Redbud	*C. racemosa*	30 feet to 10° F.	Probably the most beautiful redbud, but rarely available. Rose-colored flowers in beautiful clusters, good yellow autumn color.
Judas-tree	*C. siliquastrum*	30 feet to 0° F.	The European Redbud, similar to the American species, but leaves heart-shaped. Tree with nice, flat-top form, but no autumn color.
Chinese Fringetree	*Chionanthus retusus*	20 feet to -10° F.	An open, nearly globe-shaped tree with a fine display of white flowers in spring. Modest yellow fall color. This lilac relative, as other fringe-trees, is subject to lilac borer and to scale attacks, but worth maintaining as a specimen.
Fringetree	*C. virginicus*	30 feet to -15° F.	A native species, very showy in flower, and fragrant. As the above, with sexes on different plants. Both produce blue fruits on the female trees, males have showier flowers. Leaves larger on this, to 8 inches long, and brief fall color 'is bright yellow.

Common Name	Botanical Name	Ultimate Height Hardy	Comment
Lily-of-the-valley Clethera	*Clethera arborea*	25 feet to 25° F.	An evergreen species, leaves 3 to 4 inches long, with small, white, fragrant flowers in drooping clusters. From Madeira. Does not tolerate dry air.
Buttercup-tree	*Cochlospermum vitifolium*	20 feet to 40° F.	A Central American species, with brilliant yellow, cup-shaped blossoms. Blooms in winter. Prune after flowering to thin the top when necessary. The popular double-flowered form is seedless.
Alternate-leaved Dogwood	*Cornus alternifolia*	25 feet to -25° F.	A native species, rather non-descript; flowers, fruit, and foliage not ornamental. Mentioned only because some nurseries sell it. Apt to sucker freely. Prune lightly when inner branches begin to crowd. Subject to a leaf blight that may kill mature specimens.
Flowering Dogwood	*C. florida*	40 feet to -20° F.	One of the most beautiful native trees, with white, pink, rose, and double-flowered forms and selections with variegated leaves, or upright or weeping habit. Prune only when necessary for clearance. Subject to a trunk borer that may be destructive, to a relatively unimportant twig borer, and on occasion to scale insects.
Japanese Dogwood	*C. kousa and C. k.* 'Chinensis'	25 feet to -10° F.	A fine species, blooming later than the Flowering Dogwood and with less fall color (still good) but with showy, strawberry-pink fruits. Possibly subject to the same ills as the above, but not as frequently attacked.
Cornelian-cherry	*C. mas*	25 feet to -25° F.	A European species, low-branching and widely globe-shaped, with clouds of tiny yellow flowers in late winter or early spring, and handsome red fruits in late summer. Fall color is reddish.
Gray Dogwood	*C. racemosa*	15 feet to -25° F.	Another native species, non-descript the year round, and apt to sucker badly. Sold by some nursery companies, but should be avoided.
Cockspur Thorn	*Crataegus crus-galli*	35 feet to -20° F.	A glossy-leaved native hawthorn, forming a wide roundish head with branch tips descending almost to the ground. Prune while young to thin main branches, when older to maintain a uniform crown. Thorny, subject to cedar-apple rust and apple scab. Fruits attractive, but no appreciable fall color.

Common Name	Botanical Name	Ultimate Height Hardy	Comment
Lavalle Hawthorn	C. x *lavallei*	25 feet to -20° F.	An attractive hybrid with showy heads of white flowers and conspicuous brick-red fruits that cling over winter. Bronze-red fall color. This is subject to the same ills as the Cockspur Thorn.
Single-seed Hawthorn	C. *monogyna*	30 feet to -15° F.	Relatively intolerant of hot, dry summers and very susceptible to fire blight, this European form has little to offer American gardeners but an attractively lobed leaf. No fall color.
English Hawthorn	C. *oxyacantha*	18 feet to -20° F.	With handsome pink or red, single or double flowers (there is a double white sort) and showy red haws in the fall. Round headed, no fall color, and sensitive to heat and drought. Several good cultivars for northern climates.
Washington Thorn	C. *phaenopyrum*	30 feet to -25° F.	A good native, rather columnar when young but opens out to a dense, high, round-headed tree with age. Prune as little as possible as this throws watersprouts freely. Good flowers in late spring, showy heads of orange-red fruits in fall and winter, and good fall color. Not too susceptible to blights.
Quince	*Cydonia oblonga*	25 feet to -20° F.	This is the common, edible quince. The oblong leaves, felted beneath, are 3 to 4 inches long; flowers, 2 inches across, are white or pink; and yellow fruit ripens in late fall. A craggy, open-headed, rather flat-topped tree with considerable character. For table use plant the cultivar, 'Orange.'
Russian-olive	*Elaeagnus angustifolius*	25 feet to -40° F.	A very hardy but short-lived tree with narrow leaves 2 to 3 inches long, and bright silvery white. A gnarled tree, needing careful pruning to accent its irregular growth habit. Often suffers from a bacterial blight that wilts and kills new shoots in late spring.
Loquat	*Eriobotrya japonica*	20 feet to 10° F.	This semi-tropical tree is open branched, and with large leaves: about 2 to 3 by 7 to 10 inches, evergreen, and with a rather drooping habit. Flowers small, white; fruits pear-shaped, orange-yellow, edible. A good tree with few problems.

NOTE: Many other hawthorns are available locally, all more or less similar in growth pattern to some of the above species and hybrids. Watch for disease susceptibility.

Common Name	Botanical Name	Ultimate Height Hardy	Comment
Coral Gum	*Eucalyptus torquata*	20 feet to 30° F.	An upright, open small tree usually with several trunks. Bears masses of rose-coral buds opening to red flowers in summer. A fine tree where hardy.
Korean Evodia	*Evodia daniellii*	25 feet to -10° F.	Small, round-headed tree, rather non-descript. Attractive, fragrant small white flowers in midsummer and showy seeds and capsules in the fall. Little fall color.
Franklinia	*Franklinia alatamaha*	30 feet to -10° F.	A beautiful, rather formal tree with a round head of glossy green leaves and with 3-inch white blossoms in the fall. The autumn color is fine, orange and red. Not an easy tree for inland climates.
Moraine Ash	*Fraxinus holotricha* 'Moraine'	35 feet to -10° F.	This German species is hardy, virtually disease free and with good, upright growth. The cultivar, 'Moraine,' is almost seedless. No showy bloom or strong fall color, but a reliable tree with a suitable shape for small property.
Maries' Ash	*F. mariesii*	25 feet to 10° F.	A small Chinese ash with small, attractive leaves and handsome, barely furrowed bark. Prune while young to develop an open scaffold of main branches. Purplish autumn color.
Shamel Ash	*F. uhdei*	30 feet to 30° F.	An evergreen ash from Mexico, leaves glossy, crown almost ball-shaped. While young prune all new shoots back halfway in midsummer as this species overgrows. Older specimens are no trouble, and very ornamental.
Carolina Silverbell	*Halesia carolina*	30 feet to -5° F.	A small, sparse, native Southeastern tree that blooms with the azaleas. The small, bell-shaped blossoms are a good feature; the tree is non-descript through the rest of the season.
Mountain Silverbell	*H. monticola*	45 feet to -10° F.	A taller species than the Carolina Silverbell, with showier flowers in spring and bright yellow fall color. May become quite a tall specimen under ideal conditions, but commonly of small stature.

Common Name	Botanical Name	Ultimate Height Hardy	Comment
Kafir-plum	*Harpephyllum caffrum*	35 feet to 40° F.	An evergreen South African species, very formal and with elegant, dark green foliage. Small, rather inconspicuous flowers, and handsome dark red fruits of great ornamental value. Prune to accent the symmetrical form.
Sea-buckthorn	*Hippophae rhamnoides*	30 feet to -25° F.	A willow-like shrubby tree with silvery leaves much used for seashore planting due to its salt tolerance. Showy clusters of small orange fruits on female trees in late summer and fall. Needs considerable thinning; prune away all sprouts that appear on main trunks.
Japanese Raisin Tree	*Hovenia dulcis*	30 feet to -10° F.	An irregular-growing tree with glossy, oval leaves of good ornamental value, small white flowers, and unusual fruiting habit. Deserves wider use.
Possum-haw	*Ilex decidua*	30 feet to -15° F.	A fine native holly, deciduous, with a brushy, round head and, usually, several trunks. Plant both sexes for showy crop of fruits on female trees. No fall color except berry-covered twigs. New cultivars superior to wild stock.
Chinese Flame-tree	*Koelreuteria formosana*	40 feet to 25° F.	An upright tree with a loose, pyramidal crown. Large, lacy leaves are twice compound. Fine summer display of yellow flowers and fall display of salmon, papery pods. No fall foliage color.
Golden Rain-tree	*K. paniculata*	40 feet to -10° F.	Like the Chinese species, but flowers showier and pods pale green, drying to light brown. Seedlings may become a problem. Both species almost free of diseases and insects.
Waterer's Laburnum	*Laburnum* x *watereri*	30 feet to -10° F.	A short-lived leguminous tree with greenish gold bark, locust-like foliage, and of great ornamental value while the dangling clusters of golden blossoms appear. No fall color. Apt to canker where summers are hot and intolerant of wind. Do not prune.
Crape-myrtle	*Lagerstroemia indica*	25 feet to 10° F.	Almost always with multiple trunks, beautifully mottled, and an open, umbrella-like crown. Fine summer display of blossoms, little fall color. A good ornamental the year round.

Common Name	Botanical Name	Ultimate Height Hardy	Comment
Japanese Privet	*Ligustrum japonicum*	20 feet to 10° F.	Both this and the following, Glossy Privet, species usually are grown as shrubs but both may be pruned to single or multiple-trunked trees. Leaves evergreen, glossy, dark; flowers small and white, in terminal clusters. A trouble free plant.
Glossy Privet	*L. lucidum*	30 feet to 10° F.	Much like the above but grows taller, with leaves to 5 inches. Various cultivars with variegated leaves or glossier green leaves are listed for both sorts. Prune to open the dense crowns of all privets.
Anise Magnolia	*Magnolia salicifolia*	30 feet to -10° F.	With narrow leaves rarely attaining 4 inches in length and cup-sized white flowers in spring before leaves appear, this is a good tree for home use. The crown is pyramidal, dense. Fall color is negligible.
Saucer Magnolia	*M. x soulangiana*	25 feet to -10° F.	A low-branching, globe-shaped magnolia often with multiple trunks. Leaves and large pink and white blossoms in early spring are somewhat out of proportion to a small garden but the trouble-free tree holds its popularity. There are many cultivars of this.
Veitch Magnolia	*M. x veitchii*	30 feet to 20° F.	An English hybrid, deciduous, with lovely pink blossoms in early spring followed by quite large, handsome leaves.
Watson Magnolia	*M. x watsoni*	30 feet to -5° F.	A choice hybrid with leaves to 5 inches and pink, saucer-like flowers each with a ring of crimson stamens, borne in mid-summer. A choice species that deserves wider use.
Wilson Magnolia	*M. wilsonii*	25 feet to 0° F.	A Chinese magnolia with fragrant cup-sized, pendulous white flowers in spring and a second crop in late summer. Six inch long leaves.
Crabapples	*Malus* species and hybrids variable	to at least -10° F.	More than 200 cultivars and species of crabapples are available to American gardeners. They vary considerably in their ornamental value. Look beyond the brief display of spring flowers and consider form, foliage, disease resistance, fruit display, and in a few cases, fall color.

NOTE: Several other magnolias of small stature are valuable under rather local circumstances.

Common Name	Botanical Name	Ultimate Height Hardy	Comment
Chile Mayten-tree	*Maytenus boaria*	35 feet to 25° F.	From Chile, this pendulous-branched tree bears glossy evergreen leaves about 1¼ inches long. It is a reliable but not distinguishable tree, trouble-free, for sub-tropical areas.
Cherries and Plums	*Prunus* species and hybrids variable		Ornamental cherries, plums, peaches, chokecherries, and almonds almost all are rather short-lived, high maintenance trees. A few of the toughest and best-appearing sorts are listed.
Blireiana Plum	*P. x blireiana*	25 feet to -10° F.	Profuse, small pink flowers in early spring, coppery-purple foliage throughout summer.
'Hally Jolivette' Cherry	*P. subhirtella* hybrid	15 feet to -10° F.	With rather scruffy bark and a too dense, twiggy head, this remains popular for the fine display of pink buds and white flowers that open over about three weeks.
Pissard Plum	*P. cerasifera* 'Atropurpurea'	25 feet to -30° F.	Much like the above, but flowers and foliage less effective. Hardier.
Oriental Cherry	*P. serrulata*	25 feet to -10° F.	These are the many fine Japanese flowering cherries. Most are too broad-spreading for the small home garden, but the upright-growing cultivar, 'Amanogawa,' fits a small property.
Callery Pear	*Pyrus calleryana*	30 feet to -15° F.	A narrowly pyramidal, low branching tree with silvery bark and extremely glossy foliage. Good clusters of white flowers in spring, fruit neglible, and brilliant, long lasting red autumn color. The cultivar, 'Bradford,' is superior to the very good species. These trees are almost troublefree.
Evergreen Pear	*P. kawakamii*	30 feet to 25° F.	A straggly tree with fine, fragrant white flowers and unusual evergreen leaves that are pointed at both ends. Prune frequently when young to develop an attractive scaffold; thereafter, head back unruly branches.
Engler's Oak	*Quercus engleriana*	30 feet to 20° F.	This is a fine, Chinese evergreen oak with smallish, lustrous leaves and a pleasing growth habit.
Glandbearing Oak	*Q. glandulifera*	45 feet to -5° F.	A stately, formal tree from the Orient, open branching, with lustrous green leaves that hang on late. No fall color.

Common Name	Botanical Name	Ultimate Height Hardy	Comment
Lebanon Oak	*Q. libani*	30 feet to -10° F.	An oak that tends to be evergreen in favorable climates. Leaves about half an inch wide and 2 to 4 inches long. No fall color, but a very fine appearing tree
American Mountain-ash	*Sorbus americana*	30 feet to -40° F.	An attractive, lacy-looking small tree grown almost entirely for its fine display of bright red fruits in late summer, fall and early winter. Blights badly where summers are hot.
Folgner Mountain-ash	*S. folgneri*	25 feet to -10° F.	A smallish, upright tree, leaves dark green above, wooly white beneath. Fruits red. An attractive species, not too tolerant of heat.
Stewartia	*Stewartia* species variable	some to -10° F.	While some Stewartias tend to be shrubby, all of the Oriental and some native sorts can be pruned to single or multiple-trunked trees. Valuable for the attractive foliage, beautiful, cup-shaped white flowers in late summer, and fine red and orange autumn foliage display. Oriental sort also have attractive bark. Most fairly disease free.
Japanese Tree Lilac	*Syringa amurensis* 'Japonica'	30 feet to -15° F.	A true lilac growing usually, tree-form with a single trunk. Deciduous, usually with a tiered, rounded crown, this blooms with great cone-shaped, creamy-white flower clusters in early summer. No fall color.
Black-haw	*Viburnum prunifolium*	15 feet to -20° F.	A gnarled-appearing, small native tree with handsome glossy, deciduous leaves, and in late spring flat clusters of white flowers followed by blue-black fruits. The foliage colors a beautiful red in autumn. One of the most ornamental and least troublesome of the very small trees.
Southern Black-haw	*V. rufidulum*	30 feet to -5° F.	Very similar to the above species but larger growing. Has all the same good features.
Jujube	*Zizyphus jujuba*	30 feet to -10° F.	Hardier than commonly believed, this very irregular little tree with sparse foliage on a twiggy, tiered, globular crown, produces nondescript flowers and interesting, date-like fruits. No fall color. Tolerant of heat, drought, and alkaline soil. Old fruiting specimens occur as far north as Kansas City.

NOTE: Several other species and hybrid forms of mountain-ash are favored in various parts of the Country, especially the selected cultivars of the European Mountain-ash.

Trees for Shade

Most familiar shade trees grow to be far too large for the average city lot. They are out of proportion with low, sprawling modern houses. Think beyond the usual sugar and Norway maples, white, pin, bur, shingle, red and black oaks, lindens of several sorts, sycamores and all of the rest of the huge trees. A vase-shaped or umbrella-topped tree of only thirty feet is a good shade tree as long as it is trimmed high for head room. More information about the trees in the following list is found in the master table beginning on Page 65.

Acer carpinifolium, Hornbeam Maple

A. mandshuricum, Manchurian Maple

A. tataricum, Tatarian Maple

Bauhinia blakeana, Hong Kong Orchid Tree

B. monandra, Butterfly Bauhinia

B. purpurea, Purple Bauhinia

B. variegata, Orchid-tree

Cercis canadensis, Redbud

C. racemosa, Raceme Redbud

C. siliquastrum, Judas-tree

Crataegus crus-galli, Cockspur Thorn

C. x lavallei, Lavalle Hawthorn

C. monogyna, Single-seed Hawthorn

C. oxyacantha, English Hawthorn

C. phaenopyrum, Washington Thorn

Elaeagnus angustifolius, Russian-olive

Evodia daniellii, Korean Evodia

Fraxinus holotricha 'Moraine', Moraine Ash

F. mariesii, Maries' Ash

F. uhdei, Shamel Ash

Halesia monticola, Mountain Silverbell

Harpephyllum caffrum, Kafir-plum

Hovenia dulcis, Japanese Raisin Tree

Koelreuteria formosana, Chinese Flame-tree

K. paniculata, Golden Rain-tree

Lagerstroemia indica, Crape-myrtle

Magnolia salicifolia, Anise Magnolia

M. x veitchii, Veitch Magnolia

M. x watsoni, Watson Magnolia

M. wilsonii, Wilson Magnolia

Malus species and cultivars, Flowering Crabapples

Maytenus boaria, Chile Mayten-tree

Prunus species and cultivars, Ornamental Cherries, Plums, and Apricots

Pyrus kawakamii, Evergreen Pear

Quercus engleriana, Engler's Oak

Q. glandulifera, Glandbearing Oak

Q. libani, Lebanon Oak

Sorbus americana, American Mountain-ash

S. folgneri, Folgner Mountain-ash

Syringa amurensis 'Japonica,' Japanese Tree Lilac

Viburnum rufidulum, Southern Black-haw

Trees for Autumn Color

Many of the larger-growing, familiar shade trees, such as sugar maple, various oaks, sweetgum, and others are famous for fall color. But the traditional "shade tree" is too large for the modern city garden.

Try a smaller, brilliant-coloring sort from the list below.

Acer buergerianum, Trident Maple

A. circinatum, Vine Maple

A. ginnala, Amur Maple

A. mandshuricum, Manchurian Maple

A. nikoense, Nikko Maple

A. palmatum, Japanese Maple

A. tataricum, Tatarian Maple

Carpinus caroliniana, American Hornbeam

Chionanthus virginicus, Fringetree

Cornus florida, Flowering Dogwood

C. kousa, Japanese Dogwood

C. mas, Cornelian-cherry

Crataegus phaenopyrum, Washington Thorn

Franklinia alatamaha, Franklinia

Fraxinus mariesii, Maries' Ash

Pyrus calleryana, Callery Pear

Stewartia species, Stewartia

Viburnum prunifolium, Black-haw

V. rufidulum, Southern Black-haw

Trees with Showy Flowers

Flowers of some of the most familiar shade trees are so insignificant as to go generally unnoticed. But some trees suitable for shade in town gardens flower beautifully. Flowering trees for shade and for ornamental use in the city garden are listed below; refer to the master list on page 65 for more details about each of these.

Bauhinia blakeana, Hong Kong Orchid Tree

B. monandra, Butterfly Bauhinia

B. purpurea, Purple Bauhinia

B. variegata, Orchid-tree

Cercis canadensis, Redbud

C. occidentalis, California Redbud

C. racemosa, Raceme Redbud

C. siliquastrum, Judas-tree

Chionanthus retusus, Chinese Fringetree

C. virginicus, Fringetree

Clethera arborea, Lily-of-the-valley Clethera

Cochlospermum vitifolium, Buttercup-tree

Cornus florida, Flowering Dogwood

C. kousa, Japanese Dogwood

C. mas, Cornelian-cherry

Crataegus crus-galli, Cockspur Thorn

C. x lavallei, Lavalle Hawthorn

C. monogyna, Single-seed Hawthorn

C. oxyacantha, English Hawthorn

C. phaenopyrum, Washington Thorn

Cydonia oblonga, Quince

Eriobotrya japonica, Loquat

Eucalyptus torquata, Coral Gum

Evodia daniellii, Korean Evodia

Franklinia alatamaha, Franklinia

Halesia carolina, Carolina Silverbell

H. monticola, Mountain Silverbell

Koelreuteria formosana, Chinese Flame-tree

K. paniculata, Golden Rain-tree

Laburnum x *watereri*, Waterer's Laburnum

Lagerstroemia indica, Crape-myrtle

Magnolia salicifolia, Anise Magnolia

M. x *soulangiana*, Saucer Magnolia

M. x *veitchii*, Veitch Magnolia

M. x *watsoni*, Watson Magnolia

M. wilsonii, Wilson Magnolia

Malus species and cultivars, Flowering Crabapples

Prunus species and cultivars, Ornamental Plums, Cherries, and Apricots

Pyrus calleryana, Callery Pear

P. kawakamii, Evergreen Pear

Stewartia species, Stewartia

Syringa amurensis 'Japonica,' Japanese Tree Lilac

Viburnum prunifolium, Black-haw

V. rufidulum, Southern Black-haw

Trees with Colorful Fruit

Most trees bloom and produce seed-containing fruits; these may be dry and papery as those of maples and birches, or they may be fleshy as those of dogwood, mountain-ash, or flowering crabapple. A tree with fleshy fruits goes on the lawn, not near a walk, drive or flowerbed. Refer to the master list on page 65 for more information about the fruiting trees listed here.

Acer buergerianum, Trident Maple

Chionanthus retusus, Chinese Fringetree

C. virginicus, Fringetree

Cornus florida, Flowering Dogwood

C. kousa, Japanese Dogwood

C. mas, Cornelian-cherry

Crataegus crus-galli, Cockspur Thorn

C. x *lavallei*, Lavalle Hawthorn

C. monogyna, Single-seed Hawthorn

C. oxyacantha, English Hawthorn

C. phaenopyrum, Washington Thorn

Cydonia oblonga, Quince

Elaeagnus angustifolius, Russian-olive

Eriobotrya japonica, Loquat

Evodia daniellii, Korean Evodia

Harpephyllum caffrum, Kafir-plum

Hippophae rhamnoides, Sea-buckthorn

Ilex decidua, Possum-haw

Koelreuteria formosana, Chinese Flame-tree

K. paniculata, Golden Raintree

Malus species and cultivars, Flowering Crabapples

Prunus species and cultivars, Ornamental Plums, Cherries, and Apricots

Pyrus calleryana, Callery Pear

Syringa amurensis 'Japonica,' Japanese Tree Lilac

Viburnum prunifolium, Black-haw

V. rufidulum, Southern Black-haw

Zizyphus jujuba, Jujube

Trees not to plant*

Some trees should not be considered for the residential landscape. They are too rank, too invasive, too unattractive, or too disease-prone. Many of these are promoted by unscrupulous mailorder dealers or by "fast buck" nursery operators. The list of trees generally considered to be "weed trees" includes:

Acer negundo, box-elder. This compound-leaved maple is a fast growing, fast dying tree with surface roots, extremely weak wood, and a habit of producing myriads of almost indestructible seedlings over a wide area.

Acer saccharinum, silver, or soft maple. With an attractive leaf, this maple, like the above, is surface rooted, with exceptionally brittle wood. Quickly growing to vast size, this maple soon is disproportionate to all but the largest estate gardens.

Ailanthus altissima, tree-of-heaven. Fast-growing, highly productive of virtually indestructible seedlings, and foul smelling when bruised, there is almost no good thing to say about this invasive tree. Planting it is prohibited in some cities.

Celtis occidentalis, hackberry. This rough, insect and disease-prone tree still shows up on some recommended tree lists. But it has little ornamental merit and many bad characteristics. Surely you can find something else. Hackberry is surface rooted; the foilage is host, among others, to the nipple gall insect and to hackberry midge. Witches-broom disease disfigures the twig structure. There is no noticeable bloom and no fall color.

McClura pomifera, Osage-orange, or hedge-apple. With a gnarled but inelegant growth habit, this invasive species is thorny, with leaves making a blackish mess following the first frost. The highly invasive, surface roots are sure to pry up the sidewalk and the driveway.

Melia azedarach, Chinaberry. Once, every rural cottage and chickenyard in Oklahoma featured this species because nothing else then available was nearly as hardy. Today, better species adorn the Great Plains. Chinaberry is not a bad appearing tree, but it is invasive, and the fruits, attractive to children, are poisonous.

Morus alba and *M. rubra*, white (Tatarian), and red mulberry. With surface roots that exclude all other plant material within reach, these awkward-looking trees also produce vast amounts of fruits attractive to birds, which results in seedlings over the entire neighborhood. Only the weeping mulberry ever was very popular for garden use, and now you can plant the cultivar, 'Chaparrel,' which is fruitless.

Populus alba, white poplar, abele. This has even been called white-maple. It is a rather handsome tree with an unbelievably wide-spread root system that suckers freely.

Populus deltoides, cottonwood. This, and other cottonwoods, are fast-growing, fast dying trees with invasive, water-demanding roots, an exceptionally messy leaf fall; the female trees produce vast amounts of "cotton" as a seed dispersal means.

Sapindus drummondii, soapberry. Fortunately not much planted any longer in the southern Great Plains, this once was fairly popular. But the tree is non-descript, and the sap and fruits, when handled, cause a dermatitis resembling poison ivy rash.

Salix species. Almost all willows are too large for the modern garden, and their water-demanding, invasive roots choke the drains and sewers, invade the beds and borders, and destroy the lawn. The wood of willows is weak and brittle, and most willows are quite disease-prone.

Ulmus pumila, Siberian (Chinese) elm. This is a fast-growing, very brittle elm with no grace of character, an invasive surface root system, and productive of vast quantities of invasive seedlings. The true Chinese elm, not commonly marketed, is *U. parviflora*, quite a well-behaved species.

Fast-growing is the phrase that usually sells undesirable trees. A fast-growing tree is a fast-dying, weak-wooded tree usually with an invasive root system. Plant a fine quality shade or ornamental tree in a well spaded hole with good drainage, water it when necessary through the first year, and thereafter, push it if you wish with tree fertilizer. Even the slowest oak can be encouraged to step right along when once established.

Gardeners growing trees in treeless areas may take umbrage at this list. Some of these trees, considered to be weedy where soil is deep and weather is relatively mild, are all that will grow where rainfall is scant, soil is alkaline, and the wind blows constantly. But under those conditions, these are not weed trees because the stringent quality of the environment slows them down and prevents excessive seed production. Of course, there still will be the problem with surface roots demanding more than their share of fertility and water, but on the plains, any tree is better than no tree.

Problems with trees

Even the most beautiful tree may have some drawback, some characteristic that makes trouble for the gardener even though its many good qualities keep it in the trade. The following comments relate to these undesirable qualities.

Acer, the maples. Among the most valuable of ornamental trees, almost all maples are nearly surface-rooted, making gardening beneath the reach of their branches difficult. Even grass does not grow too well below some maples. The European sorts have no fall color of quality.

Betula, the birches. Birches, in general, are short-lived and subject to various ills, including susceptibility to borer attack. Birches are very shallow-rooted and voracious.

Crataegus, the hawthorns. Most are thorny, many are very susceptible to cedar-apple rust and some to apple scab, while some are shallow-rooted.

Elaeagnus, the oleasters. Russian-olive, particularly, is susceptible to a bacterial twig die-back.

Euonymus, the wahoo and spindle-tree. These deciduous tree-forms of Euonymus are exceptionally susceptible to attack by Euonymus scale.

Fagus, the beeches. Even these beautiful trees have drawbacks; their surface roots prevent anything from growing beneath their branches, and their precocious budding habit limits their range where intermittent late freezes occur.

Fraxinus, the ashes. Most of these are brittle, losing large limbs to high wind; many produce prodigious crops of unattractive flowers and undesirable seeds.

Gleditsia, the honeylocusts. Most are extremely thorny and produce great crops of extremely unattractive seed pods.

Juglans, the walnuts and butternuts. These attract squirrels and small boys, and the leaves and roots produce a substance which inhibits the growth of certain species, including tomatoes and hydrangeas.

Koelreuteria, the Golden Rain-trees. Members of this genus produce quantities of seed that germinate into crops of unwanted seedlings; these trees are rather shallow-rooted.

Liquidambar, the Sweetgum. A fine, large tree with many good qualities, but often with surface roots unless growing in deep, rich, damp loam.

Liriodendron, the tulip-tree. Like the Liquidambar, this genus develops shallow, extremely invasive roots.

Magnolia. The leaves of some of these pose a problem, being large and decay-resistant. Many magnolias are quite shallow-rooted. The bullbay breaks easily.

Malus, the flowering crabapples. Most of these require rather stringent pruning to maintain a clean, uncrowded crown of well-spaced branches; many are quite susceptible to cedar-apple rust and

to apple scab. Some are short-lived where summers are hot.

Platanus, the sycamores and plane-trees. The American sycamore sheds leaves and bark throughout summer and fall. Leaves of all sycamores are decay-resistant and difficult to dispose of.

Populus, the poplars and cottonwoods. These usually are brittle, short-lived, and with shallow, very invasive roots.

Prunus, the cherries, plums, and peaches. Generally these are not long-lived, some have very shallow roots, and all are subject to a host of insects, including borers. Many require considerable pruning at frequent intervals to maintain clean, open heads.

Sorbus, the mountain-ashes. Most of these are quite subject to spider-mite attack; most are limited in range, not tolerant of warm summers or hot wind.

Tilia, the lindens. These are rather shallow-rooted, their shade may be too dense to allow other ornamentals to grow nearby, and the leaves blacken and fall with the first frost.

Ulmus, the elms. Dutch-elm disease prevents recommending most of the worthwhile elms; the too commonly planted *Ulmus pumila*, mislabeled Siberian elm, is a weedy, invasive tree with a few good features and a host of bad, including surface roots, voluminous seed production, and susceptibility to storm damage.

CHAPTER 11
More about systemics

safely and effectively. It is hard to say which of the two brief statements is more important.

> **1. Read instructions carefully and follow all recommendations exactly.**
>
> **2. Never allow any trace of a systemic chemical to reach your skin or lungs.**

Systemic chemicals for shade and ornamental trees

The term "systemic" refers in most cases to insect and disease control chemicals intended for horticultural applications. Obviously, any chemical that enters the inner tissues of a living organism, plant or animal, and performs its function from that location is properly termed a "systemic." For many years insecticides and fungicides were sprayed or dusted onto the exterior of plants. They functioned from outside the plant. We still use many materials in this manner; in fact, the greatest number of our modern insecticides and disease control chemicals are applied externally to plants, and they remain outside the plant.

But a few decades ago a new family of insecticides appeared. These compounds were closely akin to certain substances that occur naturally within plants. They could be introduced to the inner tissues of a plant with no harm. If, however, an insect gnawed on a leaf of the plant or sucked sap from its tissues, the insect was poisoned. Here was an insecticide working from within the plant. It was a systemic insecticide. Research proceeded slowly. The chemical nature of systemic insecticides makes them incredibly toxic to animal life. Many extremely effective systemic insecticides had to be abandoned long before testing and research was over because of their virulence. Modern systemic insecticides, while still extremely toxic, are safe for use by trained persons. Long after systemic insecticides had become relatively common, the first systemic fungicides were under test. This still is a very new and relatively unexplored field. Only one or two partially systemic fungicides are available for horticultural use today, but research laboratories promise more and better sorts for the future.

The most effective systemic chemicals are packaged solely for use by professionally trained horticulturists. But relatively dilute preparations of some systemic insecticides are available for home owner use. Two precautions will enable you to use these preparations

While our present laws governing insecticides, fungicides and other agricultural and horticultural chemicals make it impossible for the manufacturer to give intelligent statements about controls for specific pests and diseases, you will find some generalities dealing with dilutions and control somewhere on most labels. You will also find plenty of information regarding precautions to take (these are important and cannot be followed too closely) and a great deal more information concerning legal disclaimers by the manufacturer if you poison yourself with the material. Good gardeners often sit down with the label, extract the critical information on a note pad, and stick the data on the container. It is a good practice.

Systemic control chemicals commonly are not used in dust form for topical application to foliage and stems. Systemics come in two forms; a preparation to be diluted with water for foliar application (this may be a liquid concentrate, an emulsion, or a wettable powder) or a granular preparation, to be applied to the soil for uptake by the plant's roots. You cannot make a foliar spray out of the granular material, and you should not apply the concentrate or diluted material intended for foliar use to the soil. Trained arborists and professional horticulturists sometimes use concentrated forms of systemics for direct application into a woody plant. This method is described briefly below.

Granular forms of systemic insecticides for tree pests

Granular preparations of certain systemic insecticides are prepared by soaking up the concentrated chemical with absorbent, spongy, inert material, such as vermiculite or perlite. The chemical-carrying granules go into the soil where the insecticide reaches out to be picked up by plant roots.

The active roots of a tree lie near the dripline. The crown of a tree is rather similar to a leaky roof; some rain falls through, but much of the water that catches on the upper leaves drips downward onto lower leaves slanted outward, so the water is moved toward the extremity of the branches and most of it ends up near the outer reach of the limbs. Roots grow toward moisture and toward nutrient minerals, so the drip line of the branches is where the root action occurs. And this is where systemics should be applied.

Most technicians measure off a broad band extending from a foot or two beyond the drip line to about one-third of the way from the drip line to the trunk. They measure out the appropriate weight of granular systemic insecticide, based on the diameter of the tree, and this amount is applied in the broad band that has been defined to include most of the active roots.

Ideally, the soil to be treated should be loosely cultivated. The granular material then is distributed over the band, the soil is stirred, incorporating the chemical with the earth to prevent accidental contamination of passing pets and wildlife, and the job is done. Watering triggers the release of systemic insecticide from the granules and hair roots pick up the solution, starting it on its way through the larger roots, up the trunk, through the branches, and out to the leaves. It is a neat technique.

Where the tree stands in a lawn, the job is slightly more complicated. But it is possible to treat right through the turf. It is best if the grass is mowed and raked so the granules can sift downward to the earth, neither lying on a layer of thatch nor catching on long grass blades. Air and sunlight destroy some systemics, so they always should be moved to the root zone quickly. In any case, there is danger to pets, wildlife and people if the material lies loose in the grass. A light raking will shake down any granules trapped in the grass. Then water steadily with a very fine mist for a prolonged time. The idea is to leach as much of the chemical from the granules and into the upper few inches of the soil as possible. Heavy watering may wash the systemic from the appropriate area or may flood it down deeply into the soil beyond the reach of active roots. A slow, gentle mist does the best job. This puts the systemic insecticide into the top eight or ten inches of soil where it is readily available to tree roots.

Systemics applied in this manner give spectacular results with some difficult pests. Ornamental trees in the apple family — hawthorns, crabapples, medlars, and the like — sometimes are host to aphids overwintering in the buds, and appearing in ruinous numbers on new foliage as quickly as buds begin to open in the spring. If so, anticipate bud burst and two to three weeks before buds are due to open apply a granular systemic under the tree. If your favorite shade tree is host to difficult-to-control galls that seem to defy the tree technician's best efforts, determine the life cycle of the pest from your County Extension Agent's office and during the underground part of the pest's life cycle be there with your granular systemic. In some cases it pays to make two applications — one when the pest is leaving the tree to go into the soil, and another when the insect is due to leave the soil to begin its aboveground activities. A holly planting badly infested with leaf miner can be cleaned up entirely in a season or two if a granular systemic is applied properly just as buds begin to swell in early spring.

Take the necessary precautions when putting down granular systemics. These preparations are dusty, and that dust is toxic if you breath it or get it on your skin. Dress in clothing that can be laundered as quickly as the job is finished, and wear vinyl or rubber gloves. Do your weighing and pouring of granules in the open air, not in a closed room where dust will swirl. When the job is done, wash shoes and gloves as well as clothing.

Systemics in cartridge form

A few systemic insecticides and perhaps one fungicide can be purchased in cartridge form. The cartridges are inserted into a hose-attached root "feeding" gadget, which is nothing more than a perforated pipe; and as the water passes the cartridge, it dissolves and the material is carried in the water to the root zone where the pipe is located. The use of this sort of material is akin to the application of granular form systemic insecticides in that the chemical is applied to the soil in solution where active roots absorb it, and carry it via larger roots, trunk, and branches, to the leaves.

The cartridge method works if you follow all the necessary instructions. Count out the appropriate number of cartridges according to the instructions on the package. This number will be based on the size of the tree. Operate the instrument correctly. The perforations should be ten to fifteen inches below the surface in that broad band which includes most of the active roots. Too deep or too shallow does not get it. Use moderate water pressure so the systemic solution is distributed only in the vicinity of the perforated pipe and not pushed to the surface or forced beyond the reach of the roots. Make an insertion every two or three inches round the area to be treated so the systemic solution is evenly distributed, saturating the soil with insecticide.

Take the proper precautions. Wear rubber or vinyl gloves when handling systemic insecticide cartridges as the chemical is in concentrated form. Wash the gloves and instrument thoroughly when the job is completed. It is a good idea to set the sprinkler to wash off the grass in the treated area, too.

Systemics as foliar sprays

Insecticides applied as foliar sprays are a boon to beleaguered gardeners. When mimosa webworm attacks Japanese silk trees and honey locusts or when elm leaf beetles begin to strip green tissues from elm leaves (these are but two of many possible examples), chemical control is essential. The average topical insecticide can be expected to last from a few hours to a few days — but the plague of insects remains a threat for a greater period of time. Respraying once or twice becomes necessary.

Not so with most systemic insecticides. Choose a chemical specified for control of the insect pest at hand, make up the correct spray solution, and do a good job of applying it to your tree. Insects will begin to die soon, but the kill will continue over a prolonged period because the chemical has entered into the plant and remains as an active control chemical for four to six weeks, a period longer than the life cycle of many common pests. Aphids on hawthorns and flowering crabapple trees (among others), nipple gall midges on hackberry, gooseberry gall insects on pin oak, all these and other pests can be controlled by applying the appropriate foliar systemic insecticide at just the right time.

Throwing a mist of systemic insecticide into the air is questionable business because of the toxicity of the material. Take every precaution. Close the area to pets. Remove all toys, tools and similar items. Cover the fish pond with unbroken plastic. Cut off air intake apertures to the house and garage. Close all of the windows. Then, seal off your own skin. Don at least two layers of impervious clothing, heavy denim, sweat clothes and the like to keep the drifting mist from your skin. Rubber boots and rubber gloves complete the body protection. Add a charcoal respirator, clear plastic face mask, an old hat, and you are ready to spray. Sounds ridiculous? It isn't. The nature of most systemics make them able to enter your body directly through the skin. You don't have to swallow the chemical, breath it, or pour it on your skin. If the vapor reaches you, in it goes. Spraying systemics down low and in a restricted area, as when treating the roses, is one thing. Throwing a drifting mist high into a tree with your pressure sprayer or trombone sprayer is something else. Some of it is almost sure to come your way. Be prepared; be covered. When the spray job is finished, rinse the sprayer quickly and leave the thorough cleaning for a few minutes. Get out of those mist-dampened clothes — put them right into the washing machine with bleach and detergent — and then go back and properly flush and clean the sprayer.

Systemic insecticide sprays are one of the most efficient tools to use on ornamental and shade trees for controlling pests that are apt to recur over several weeks. It is best if you arrange to have your absolutely trustworthy tree man do the spraying — after you have battened the hatches as described above — but not too many tree men keep a suitable systemic on hand or apply it correctly. If you find yourself stuck for applying the systemic, take every precaution; if you do it right, safety is no problem and you will not have to spray again for six to eight weeks, if at all.

Systemic concentrates for direct injection

This is nothing for the home owner. But it is a very effective and safe way to make a tree poisonous from the inside out, and you may wish to have a licensed tree technician (arborist) do the job for you in certain cases.

The technique is as follows. Small holes are bored every two to four inches round the circumference of the tree at a convenient working height. In the old days, a special small nozzle was inserted into each hole briefly while the concentrated systemic insecticide solution was pumped under high pressure into the hole. It took quite a long time to work all around the tree.

Today a better device is used. It is a small tube that jams tightly into each hole with a small reservoir on each tube. The unit is called a Mauget cup or reservoir, and the thing looks vaguely like an old fashioned corn cob pipe refashioned out of aluminum. Obviously, some precautions are necessary when these things are applied to a large tree. There may be a dozen or more of them round the tree trunk and children may be curious about them. A knowledgeable adult ought to stand by, keeping an eye on the set-up until all of the chemical in every reservoir has been absorbed by the tree. Then a technician with heavy vinyl or rubber gloves should remove the units and take them away for safe disposal.

This direct injection technique is very neat. When a tree is leafed out hundreds of gallons of water enter through the roots each day to be moved upwards in the sapwood (the inch or two of wood just under the bark) for distribution throughout the branches, twigs, and leaves. Obviously, if a systemic insecticide in concentrated form is injected into the sap stream to be carried upward, distribution will be general throughout the tree. There is no problem with a poisonous spray drifting over the house, terrace, lawn, or fish pool. There is no problem with spray-contaminated clothing, shoes, mask, and the rest of it. There is no residue to be flushed from the frequently used home spray tank.

Are there drawbacks to direct injection using the disposable reservoirs? Drilling holes into a living tree is not the best practice in the world. Any hole is an open wound, but at least in this case the holes are small and open for only a brief period. When the tree man has removed the reservoirs, fill your calking gun with tree wound dressing and plug each hole. Probably these wounds would heal shut in a single season if left untreated, but somehow it seems a good idea to fill them. There is the matter of a tree man to do the work. You must find a licensed technician who understands the problem, is trained to drill holes to the proper depth, to space them properly, and to install the reservoirs for best results. Finally, there is the matter of guarding the treated tree until uptake is complete. During a cool, rainy spell, twenty-four hours or more may be required to empty the reservoirs, in which case only trees in enclosed gardens (safely secured from children by fencing) should be treated. On a warm, sunny, windy afternoon the reservoirs may be drained in two or three hours. You can read a garden book or hoe the petunias with one eye on the tree. When the reservoirs are empty, a phone call to the tree technician's radio dispatcher will locate a trained man to remove and carry them away. Keep your hands off them!

Today we commonly see this sort of treatment used to fight disease transmitting bark beetles of elm, oak, and certain other species. It is a sure way of destroying a crop of aphids on maple or nipple gall insects on hackberry (if the timing is right). At least one fungicide is applied in this fashion for combating Dutch elm disease. There is much to be said for direct injection of systemics, not the least of which is that the home gardener never handles the chemical.

Index

INVENTORY 1983